Rome and the Arab Rise of Islam

―――――――

A Brief Introduction

Greg Fisher

About the author

Greg Fisher is Assistant Professor in the Department of History and the College of the Humanities at Carleton University in Ottawa, Canada. He is an expert on the Near East in late antiquity and on the Arabs in the pre-Islamic period. He is the author of numerous works on the topic, including *Between Empires: Arabs, Romans, and Sasanians in Late Antiquity* (Oxford University Press, 2011), and the editor of *Arabs and Empires Before Islam* (Oxford University Press, in publication).

Acknowledgments

The research material from this book rests on a wide range of academic disciplines and sub-disciplines. I am grateful for the support and help I have received from the various experts in epigraphy, linguistics, archaeology, and others who have cleared up issues and corrected errors so that they would not appear here. Any errors that remain are mine, alone. Finally, I am grateful to my research assistant at Carleton, Katie McFarland, for her help editing and proofing the text.

Rome and the Arabs before the rise of Islam

Contents

Introduction

Maps

1: Rome, Iran, and the Arabs
2: Arabs, Empires, Christianity
3: Political and military affairs
4: New Arab allies, 497-602
5: Culture and identity
6: Continuity and change

References and further reading

Introduction

The genesis of this short book is in a course I taught in the winter of 2012 to undergraduates at Carleton University. The course, *Rome and the Arabs*, lacked an affordable and readable book directed towards undergraduates and educated non-specialists about the complex world of pre-Islamic Arabia and its relationship with the Roman Empire. So, I decided to put together a very short volume which aimed to capture the state of research in the field, and which will, I hope, provide a concise introduction to a topic which is of enduring interest. The Middle East remains firmly rooted in our headlines and many of the same problems which were relevant to the Romans – questions about faith, political allegiance, stability, and security – continue to revolve around it today.

The majority of the book concentrates on the relationship between the Arabs and the Romans, simply because the history of the Arabs in the pre-Islamic period is dominated by Roman sources. But this book also draws the Sasanian Empire of Iran into the discussion. The Sasanian Empire played an important role in the growing political and religious identity of Arabs in the pre-Islamic period, though one which is not very well understood. The term 'Sasanian' refers to the empire's ruling family, which held power between 224 and the mid-seventh century. Taking Romans, Iranians, and Arabs together, then, as much as possible, this book sets out, from an historical perspective – rather than a theological or an ideological one – the political and religious affairs of the Arabs in the period usually known as 'late antiquity,' from the end of the third century until the Muslim invasions nearly halfway through the seventh. This book does not specifically address the formation of Islam, but it does discuss and describe, to some extent, its political and cultural background as represented by the triangular relationship between Romans, Iranians, and Arabs.

The Muslim conquest of the Sasanian Empire and large portions of the eastern portion of the Roman Empire in the mid-seventh century constituted a stunning military victory. The Roman and Sasanian empires were the two superpowers of the ancient world, and their devastating defeat by the Muslim armies ushered in a new era. The new Muslim *umma*, or community, faced in towards the lands of the Middle

East, not out towards the Mediterranean Sea as the Roman world had done. This reoriented trade routes and the outlook of the region's new rulers, forever changing the relationship between Europe and the Middle East. Arabic replaced Greek as the dominant language of administration and religion. And of course a new religion, Islam, came to coexist with, and then outpace, Judaism and Christianity in the former heartlands of the Roman East – what constitutes now Jordan, Syria, Palestine, and Egypt. Yet precisely because of these momentous and world-changing events, the history of the Arabs *before* Islam is frequently ignored. The Arabs, it used to be thought, did not have an identity, or at least not much of one, before the seventh century. But many things which came to define Arab identity in the period after the emergence of Islam, such as religious allegiances, language, political action, and so on, existed beforehand as well. We know that the Arabs used Arabic, that they worshipped a variety of deities, that they had diplomatic relations with the various states around them, and some, especially in the sixth century, held positions of considerable importance as part of the Roman and Sasanian bureaucratic and military hierarchies. This short book thus covers the political role of Arabs as allies of the Roman and Sasanian empires, their religious status within both realms, and how, taken together, the slim and patchy evidence for their activities provides a portrait of the Arabs before the seventh century – before the arrival of Islam altered the course of the history of the Arabs, and the history of the region we now refer to as the Middle East.

In the first chapter, I examine the political and cultural state of play in the late antique Near East – that is, the geographical area framed by Rome's eastern provinces and the Sasanian Empire. This includes the area usually called the 'Fertile Crescent', as well as the deserts which stretched south into the Arabian Peninsula. Because almost all of the ancient source material concerning the Arabs was produced by people writing within or at the fringes of the Roman Empire, and not the Arabs themselves, it is essential to take into consideration the background and world-view against which they produced their accounts. This section will also address issues of terminology and forms of historical evidence.

The subsequent chapters will take a chronological view of the developing relations between

Rome, the Sasanians, and the Arabs, and will also address events in the Arabian Peninsula – the territory covered by modern Saudi Arabia. Finally, we will see how on the eve of Islam, the Arabs had developed an identifiable political identity as frontier allies of the two great empires; how the Arabs that allied with Rome had adopted the state religion, Christianity, providing them with a religion 'of the Book' – an Abrahamic faith – and how they provided models of Arab leadership in Syria and Jordan, well before the first Muslim Arab raiding parties encountered bewildered and stunned imperial patrols on the long-neglected southern frontier of the Roman Empire.

At the end of this short introduction I include a timeline of major events discussed in this book. All dates, unless otherwise indicated, are in AD. Finally, as is the convention with books of this sort, there are no footnotes. Instead, readers are directed towards the references and bibliography at the end of the book.

Timeline

161-169: Ruwwafa inscription erected, honouring Roman emperors Marcus Aurelius and Lucius Verus (Verus on the throne until 169)

275: Kingdom of Himyar annexes Saba, begins program of expansion of power throughout Arabian Peninsula

293: Paikuli inscription from Kurdistan reveals Amr of Lakhm as Sasanian vassal –first evidence for the Nasrid dynasty during reign of Diocletian (Rome) and Narseh (Iran)

328: Nemara inscription, Syria, honours Imru al-Qays during the reign of Constantine (Rome), and Shapur II (Iran)

375-378: Revolt by the Arab queen Mavia against the Roman emperor Valens; Valens killed in action at Adrianople (378); Mavia's forces defend Constantinople from the victorious Goths

420s: Aspebetos brings his people to St. Euthymius for conversion; Aspebetus subsequently attends Council of Ephesus (431) as bishop, 'Peter of the Parembole'

So-called *Saraceni* appear in the *Notitia Dignitatum* as army units

?mid-fifth c.: Himyarite expeditions to Ma'add probably result in installation of family of Hujr, 'Hujrids', as Himyar's deputies there

473: Arab adventurer Amorkesos quits Sasanian Empire to raid Roman territory; takes island of Iotabe for himself until c. 497

After 491: Romans work to bring Hujrids into alliance, detach them from Himyar; use Axumite (Ethiopian) kingdom as proxy to exert pressure (see 523)

497/8: Disturbances in southern Jordan probably reflect Ghassan and Jafnids entering Roman Empire; alliance formed between Jafnid leader Gabalas (?-c.528) and the Roman emperors Anastasius (491-518) and Justin I (518-527)

c. 500: Inscriptions show that a transition is occurring between the Nabataean Aramaic script and what we would think of as an identifiably Arabic script in northern Arabia – see 512

504: Al-Mundhir becomes leader of the Nasrid family at al-Hirah in Iraq, under the patronage of the Sasanian Emperor

512: Zebed inscription in Syria erected – first to be in Arabic language *and* script

520s: Religious tensions in south Arabia between Jews and Christians culminate in 'massacre of Najran'; Nasrid leader al-Mundhir approached by Himyarite leader, Dhu Nuwas, to support

521: Himyarite expedition with Kinda (including probably Hujrids) against Sasanians

523: Axumite (Ethiopian) kingdom invades Himyar

525: Possible sack of al-Hirah by Hujrids, acting under Roman influence

527/8: Ruqaym scratches his message into the volcanic crater at Jebel Seis, Syria in Arabic language and script, mentioning the future Jafnid leader and son of Gabalas, Arethas

The last Hujrid leader, al-Harith, is killed in battle against al-Mundhir

Romans intensify diplomatic efforts to manipulate leadership contests in northern central Arabia

528/9: The Roman Emperor Justinian (527-565) decides to support Arethas, Jafnid leader between 528/9 and 568, as sole Arab ally to counter the Nasrid al-Mundhir

531: Roman forces at Callinicum are defeated by the Sasanians; Arethas gets the blame

542: Arethas wins Jacob Baradeus for the monophysites in Syria and Arabia

548: Jafnid/Nasrid ambassadors join those of Romans and Sasanians in visit to Abraha of Himyar

554: Arethas finally dispatches his Nasrid nemesis al-Mundhir in battle. Series of weak and ineffectual Nasrid leaders take over

568: Harran inscription, in Arabic language and script, erected in Syria

568/9: Arethas dies; succeeded by son, Alamoundaros

572: Assassination attempt on Alamoundaros by Roman Emperor Justin II (565-578)

580: Alamoundaros in Constantinople to mediate amongst the monophysites at invitation of Roman Emperor Tiberius II (578-582)

c. 581: Failed military expedition by Roman general Maurice and Alamoundaros

582: Alamoundaros arrested and exiled to Sicily on orders of new Roman Emperor, Maurice, (582-602)

602: Final Nasrid leader al-Numan executed on orders of Sasanian Emperor Khusrau II; Khusrau initiates massive invasion of Roman Empire after Maurice is toppled by Phocas in Constantinople

604: Day of Dhu Qar – Sasanian forces defeated by Arabs near al-Hirah

610: Phocas is toppled in coup by Heraclius; the Roman fightback begins

c.628: Heraclius victorious; Khusrau II toppled

636: Roman forces beaten by Muslim armies at Yarmuk

637: Sasanian forces beaten by Muslim armies; capital, Ctesiphon, captured

651: Death of last Sasanian Emperor, Yazdegerd III

Maps

The Fertile Crescent, from G. Fisher, *Between Empires. Arabs, Romans, and Sasanians in Late Antiquity* (Oxford, 2011).

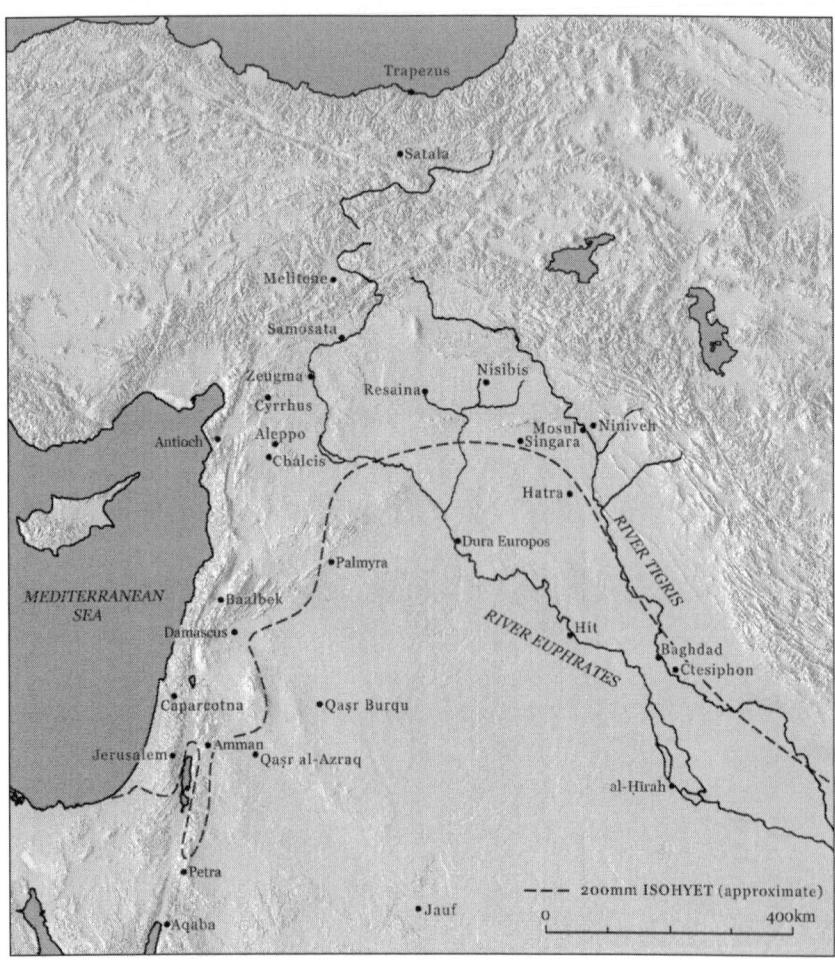

The western side of the Arabian peninsula, from G. Fisher, *Between Empires. Arabs, Romans, and Sasanians in Late Antiquity* (Oxford, 2011).

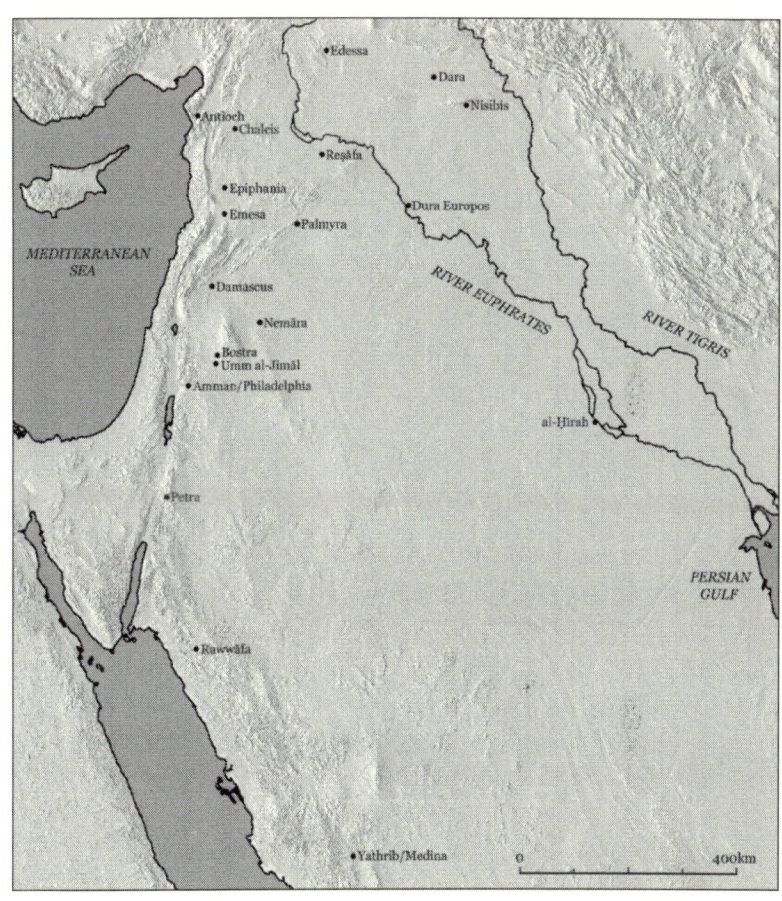

The Arabian peninsula, from G. Fisher, *Between Empires. Arabs, Romans, and Sasanians in Late Antiquity* (Oxford, 2011), after C. Robin, "Les Arabes de Himyar, des <<Romains>> et des Perses (IIIe-VIe siècles de l'ère chrétienne)," *SEC* 1 (2008), 168.

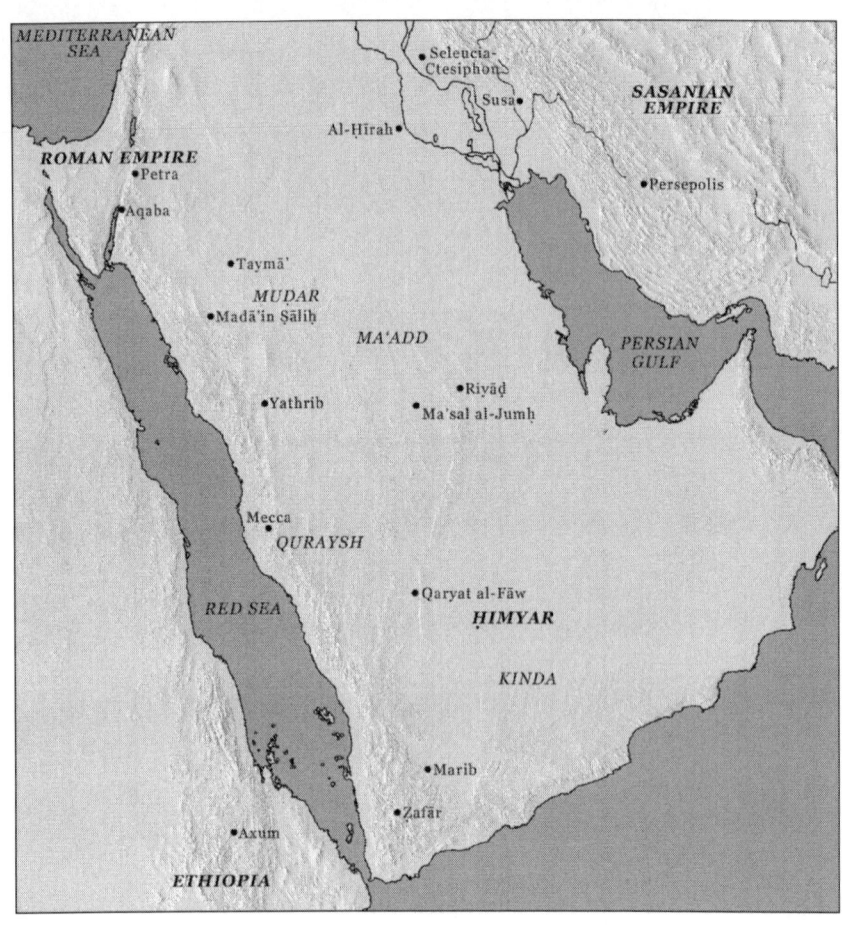

Northern Syria, showing the location of Resafa, from
G. Fisher, *Between Empires. Arabs, Romans and
Sasanians in Late Antiquity* (Oxford, 2011).

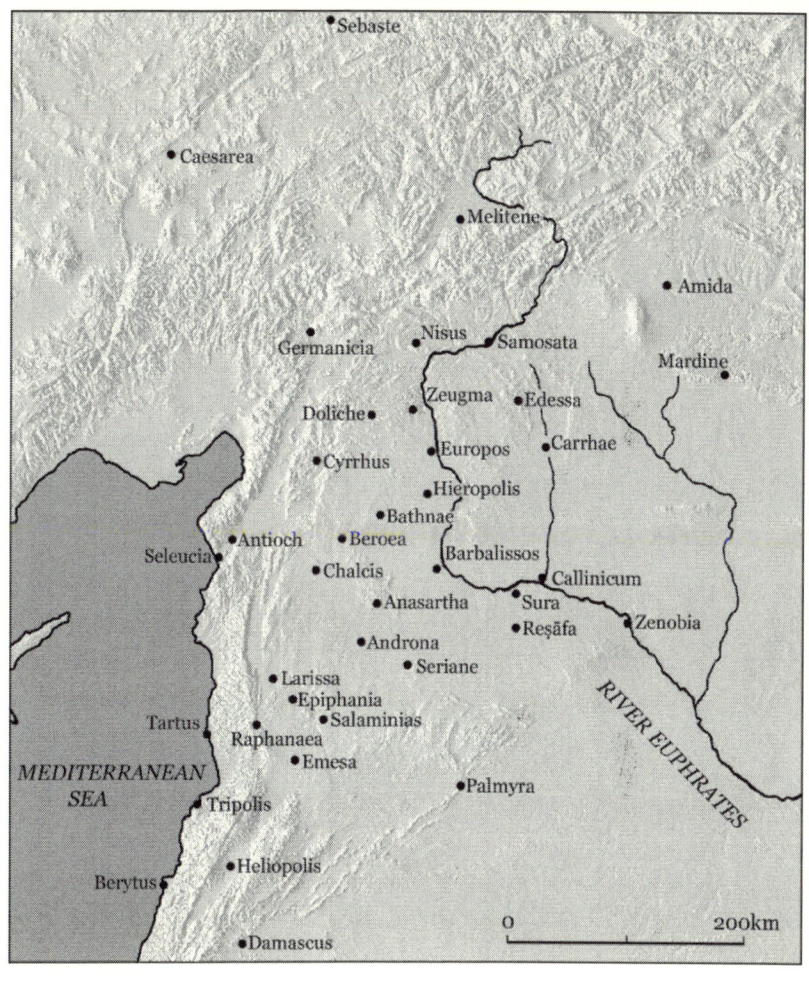

Central Syria, showing the location of Zebed, Harran, Jebel Seis, and Nemara, from G. Fisher, *Between Empires. Arabs, Romans, and Sasanians in Late Antiquity* (Oxford, 2011).

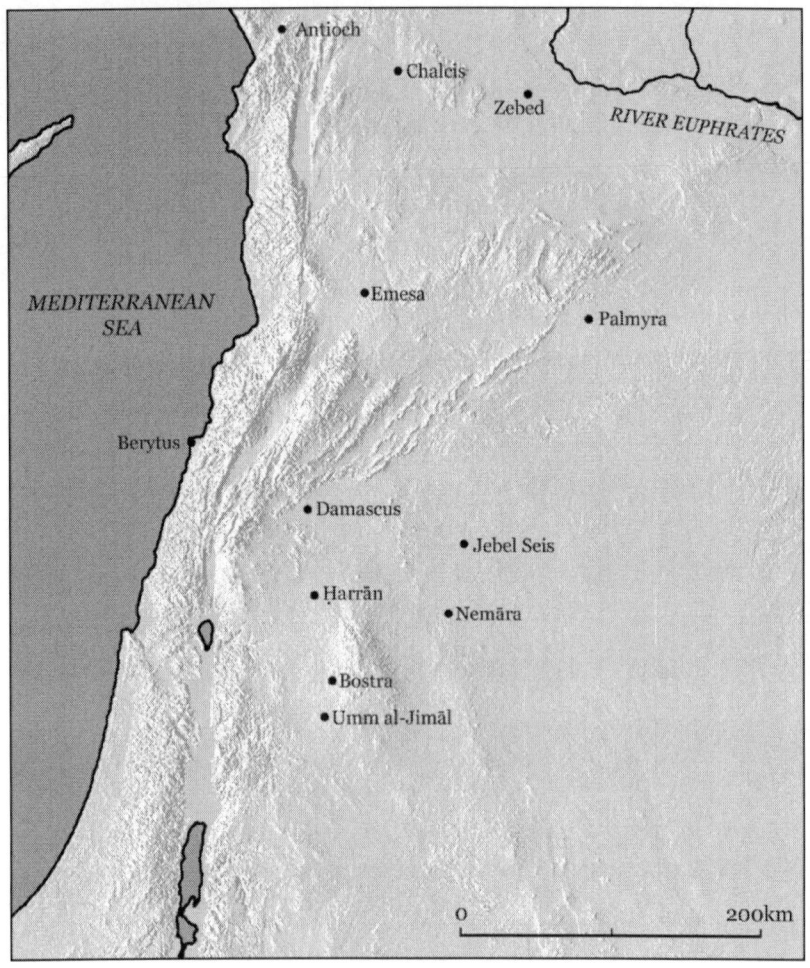

1

Rome, Iran, and the Arabs in late antiquity

Like many of the peoples who lived along the periphery of the Roman Empire – Goths, Franks, Vandals, and so on – the majority of the evidence that we have for the Arabs was produced by the Romans themselves. Roman authors followed older Greek models in providing 'ethnographies' (Greek for 'writing about people'), and such works were usually less than complimentary in their observations of 'barbarians' – people who lacked Greco-Roman civilisation. Nomads suffered particular punishment. Roman and Greek writers alike viewed their failure to settle down, live in houses, and farm cereals and vines, with great suspicion. These prejudices went back to Aristotle's *Politics*, where in his exposé of different modes of life, a mobile living was very much towards the bottom of the heap. Because Roman writers invariably understood Arabs to be nomads – even if they weren't – the portraits which they provide of the peoples they glimpsed along the desert frontiers of their vast empire were naturally unsavoury and very often hostile. And since the Arabs did not produce any written accounts of their history until well after the seventh century, it is rather difficult to reconstruct a sympathetic or neutral history of them from the range of often-biased and hostile sources that are available to us.

The preponderance of Roman material on the Arabs also means that the history of the Arabs cannot be understood in isolation. To do so would remove almost all of the historical evidence for the Arabs, and, more importantly, take the very small amount of material produced by the Arabs themselves out of the context in which it was produced. All three of the earliest examples of written Arabic in the script that we now associate with the language are from the Roman Empire, and two of them are from Christian sites, important to Arabs, but likely used by Romans and Arabs together. They are thus very much 'Roman' in character and need to be seen with that in mind. There are other reasons to keep a Roman angle in the picture. For example, in the late twentieth century, a significant effort was made by the European Science Foundation to understand how the Roman Empire's relations with the Goths, Franks, Vandals, and other Germanic peoples in western Europe helped to build the foundations of medieval Europe; now, it has proven productive to think of the Arabs in the same way. In other words, the relationship between the Romans and the Arabs, as with that between the Romans and western Germanic peoples, actually helped to build political power among the Arab élites in much the same way that Germanic warlords became kings of the early medieval states of Europe. This process could not have taken place without the support of a wealthy and powerful Empire. Because of this crucial phenomenon – a process of state-formation – it is in fact far more helpful to place the Arabs within the wider history of the region, rather than seeing them as separate from the history of the Roman Empire, or indeed any other of their neighbours. It was the Empire that delivered money, titles, Christianity, opportunities, and so on, to so many of its peripheral peoples. The leaders of these peoples, whether Arabs or Germans, were 'Romanised' in the process, but they also used what they were given to build new identities for themselves. Another aspect of this process, especially relevant to our focus on the east, is the addition of interstate conflict. In the west, the Germans really had no other powerful state to play the

Romans off against, but the Arabs were gifted with a myriad of military and political opportunities through the long rivalry between the Roman and Sasanian Empires. Similar situations existed in other periods of history. For example, the struggle for primacy in North America between England and France in the seventeenth and eighteenth centuries created similar opportunities (and obstacles) for Native American populations. In late antiquity, the two mighty superpowers of Rome and Iran fought each other to a standstill, and increasingly the Arabs acted as allies, enemies, and mediators in this conflict. The history of the Arabs in the pre-Islamic period is therefore, in the end, very much a part of Roman (and Sasanian) imperial history as well.

Rome and Iran in Late Antiquity

The Roman Empire was a very different sort of political entity than its Republican predecessor, which had operated a form of representative government until it was destroyed by the ambitions of young, powerful men, such as Julius Caesar, Mark Antony, and Octavian, who took the name Augustus as Rome's first emperor. Under Augustus, serious representative government vanished, to be replaced by the rule of one man – an imperial monarchy. The time of Augustus and his successors was one of military retrenchment until the period of the so-called 'Five Good Emperors' (Nerva, Trajan, Hadrian, Antoninus Pius, and Marcus Aurelius), at which point military opportunism and the threats of foreign enemies once more asserted themselves. It was during the rule of Trajan that the Roman Empire reached its height, and it was under him and Marcus Aurelius that the Romans finally achieved major success over the Parthian Empire, their old enemy and the predecessor of the Sasanian Empire. The Romans could not have known that the crushing victories over the Parthians in this period, when Roman armies marched through the streets of the capital of Seleucia-Ctesiphon, in modern Iraq, were due just as much to Parthian weakness as to Roman strength.

The death of Marcus Aurelius, in 180, marked the end of the 'Roman peace' (*pax Romana*) established by Augustus, an age of prosperity and stability for the Roman state. Afterwards the Roman Empire lurched from crisis to crisis, battling economic malaise, unrelenting foreign and civil wars, and a succession of ineffectual, morally vacuous, or predatory political leaders. New enemies asserted themselves, and the 'third-century crisis', as this period is often known, witnessed some of the worst defeats the Romans ever encountered. In 251, the Emperor Decius vanished into a swamp somewhere in Romania, his army ambushed and destroyed by a band of Goths. The Sasanians made their presence felt, too, defeating a Roman army near Edessa in Turkey (below).

The Roman Empire found succor under the Emperor Diocletian (r. 284-305). Diocletian restored the integrity of the Empire's borders and some semblance of order, creating a rule of four, the Tetrarchy. He later became the only Roman ruler in history to voluntarily abdicate the throne. Diocletian is said to have busied himself in retirement with the cultivation of cabbages, while the system he had painstakingly built fell apart around him. He died in 311, in the middle of yet another civil war to determine the direction of the Roman state. The eventual victor, Constantine (r. 306-337), abolished the Tetrarchy, and restored single monarchical rule after experimenting with, and abandoning, other collegial forms of government. Constantine is best known for making

Christianity the state religion, and beginning the process wherein the Emperor became the arbiter of what was deemed the 'right' sort of Christianity to follow. The Emperor now ruled on *orthodoxy* – the 'right road' – and against *heresy* – 'the wrong choice.' Constantine profoundly changed the Roman state by backing it with a universalising religion, and while religion had played a prominent role in Roman politics since the formation of the Republic in 509 BC, now, more than ever, the zeal of Christian monotheism assumed great importance. The Emperor's focus on orthodoxy was part of this, but so too was the idea that non-Roman or 'barbarian' frontier allies should be Christian. A shared, common religion was understood by the Romans to bind politically, to make the untrustworthy faithful, and to ensure reliability in the fickle. The period of Constantine's rule and after happens to coincide with increased contacts with Arabs, as the Empire looked for allies along the southeastern frontiers in what is now Jordan and Saudi Arabia. As we shall see, Christianity played an important role in these encounters, as it did anywhere the Romans tried to suborn frontier peoples and use them as military and political allies.

The adoption of Christianity as the state religion also had consequences for Rome's ancestral enemy across the Euphrates. The Empire of Iran in late antiquity was the successor to a much older institution. In the 330s BC, Alexander the Great had conquered its first incarnation, the Achaemenid Empire, which had been founded by the famous Cyrus the Great in the sixth century BC. After an interlude of Macedonian rule, many of the territories of this vast kingdom - which at times stretched from the Mediterranean Sea to Pakistan - were slowly reconstituted under a family dynasty known as the Arsacids. The Parthians, as the Arsacids are more usually known, gained fame as the 'boogeymen' of the Roman Republic. Julius Caesar's colleague Marcus Crassus had tried his strength against the Parthians in 55 BC and failed, losing his life and a great deal of his army. In a nasty homage to Crassus' legendary wealth, rumours swirled that he had been murdered by the Parthians by having molten gold poured down his throat. Caesar himself was planning an expedition of revenge when he was murdered in 44 BC. As noted above, success against the Parthians only really materialised towards the end of the second century AD.

In 224, the Arsacids were overthrown by a new dynasty, the Sasanians. The first Sasanian monarch, Ardashir I, created a kingdom that was more militarised than its predecessor, and which possessed a far more efficient administration that could harness the resources of the vast, sprawling territory which it controlled. The Sasanians also had close links with the priests of the universalising state religion, Zoroastrianism. While the religious climate of the Sasanian Empire is best considered a mosaic of different faiths and beliefs, including Christianity, Zoroastrianism lay firmly at its core. Also part of Sasanian ideology, perhaps – it is a matter of some debate – was a desire to recover the territory lost to Alexander the Great in the 330s BC. This included many of the lands now comprising the Roman provinces of Syria, Phoenicia (Lebanon), Arabia (Jordan), and so on. The Sasanians offered a new threat to the Romans: the contemporary Roman senator and historian Cassius Dio noted that the change in leadership in the east made all people, not just the Romans, fearful. But it was not just the warlike nature of the Sasanians which would ensure nearly four centuries of conflict. The juxtaposition of two world empires, both of which espoused a powerful universal religion, was not conducive to peace between the two sides of the River Euphrates, which, for much of the history of the conflict, formed the boundary between the Roman and Sasanian states. Between the third and seventh centuries, religious tensions, often linked to the status of Christians in the Sasanian Empire, sparked cross-border conflicts. Yet despite those Roman assertions that the Sasanians were hell-bent on recovering all the territory lost to Alexander, it was only in 602 that the Sasanians launched a war that seemed to have this sort of objective in mind. They eventually failed, but not until a generation of Romans from Egypt to Turkey had been raised under Sasanian occupation. While the crisis of the early seventh century was the closest Rome had come to being destroyed since the war with Hannibal, the Sasanians had inflicted other notable defeats on the Romans, most famously at Edessa in 259. There, the dynamic and aggressive Shapur I destroyed a Roman army and captured its commander, the Emperor Valerian. Valerian, like Crassus, before him, is reported to have suffered a gruesome fate. The anti-pagan Christian polemicist Lactantius, writing after the event, reported that Valerian had been skinned, and his hide hung in a prominent temple where visiting Roman ambassadors could see it, and be reminded of their shameful loss at Edessa.

Geographical considerations limited the scope of the numerous wars which took place between the accession of Constantine and the great war of 602. The vast Syrian desert provided an appalling prospect for a large army to cross from east to west, or vice versa: food was scarce, water nearly non-existent. The 'Fertile Crescent' gets its name from the curve of lush land which sits on the region like a horseshoe. Between the curve of the 'Fertile Crescent' only dry (irrigated) farming was possible, and even then only in a very small area. The rest of the desert was the preserve of mobile peoples, conventionally called nomads, who traded with the peoples of the villages and cities, and occasionally fought them. The natural invasion route then for either foe was along the fertile banks of the Euphrates River, and through Mesopotamia – southern Turkey and northern Iraq. Both Romans and Sasanians quickly established major fortresses in Mesopotamia to forestall the advances of the other, and this ensured that many wars were bogged down by long and costly sieges. The natural response of both sides to this was to look for other opportunities. But with the desert so difficult to cross, what could be done? The answer was deceptively straightforward: cultivate relations with the peoples of the periphery, such as the Tzani, Armenians, and Lazi of the Caucasus – or the peoples of the desert, the Arabs – and use them as proxies to exert pressure on one's opponent.

Who were the Arabs?

In antiquity, the term 'Arab' did not refer to a well-defined ethnicity or group membership in the way that today, 'French' or 'British' can. In these categories, we can look to certain types of 'markers' to say that person x is French and person y isn't – things like language, names, family history, culinary interests, political membership, and so on. Not all of these categories are especially helpful in antiquity, and so to speak of an 'Arab' is a difficult thing to do beyond the most basic geographical definition – someone from the land known as Arabia, i.e., modern Jordan and the deserts of Saudi Arabia. So what could 'Arab' mean in antiquity? It could refer to the geographical space just mentioned; to a pejorative idea produced by settled people of a nomadic one; in an administrative sense, as one who came from the Roman province of Arabia, whose boundaries shifted at various times in antiquity. This administrative idea is a little like calling oneself a Quebecer (from Quebec, not Ontario) or a Californian (from the place demarcated as the state of California, and not, say, from Nevada). Probably, like these two examples, it carried with it some stereotypical attributes as well, although we don't know what those might be. The term 'Arab' could also be used in contexts which defy definition: a third-century BC papyrus from Egypt refers to a certain Parates as an 'Arab', and an epitaph from the Greek island of Thasos, six hundred years later, talks of a Rufinus as an 'Arab.' In neither case can we be precisely sure what the author meant. A people? A person from Arabia? The Roman orator Cicero makes links between Arabs and skill at bird-augury, suggesting that this was a trait of 'Arabs', but Romans could be fond of such sweeping generalisations. The word 'Arab' became common in Egypt, too, where it may have acquired its own meaning connected to 'being' a nomad (another Roman-inspired generalisation). Indeed, Roman authors liked the term, since it was one the many barbarian labels available to be used to define things that were 'not Roman.' More than anything, in antiquity, what it did *not* mean was anything like what it means today, where the word 'Arab' is usually associated with the religion of Islam and with the region of the Middle East. For the purposes of this book, the Arabs are defined, non-ideologically, with a geographical definition: as people who came from the Arabian Peninsula and its environs.

Another contentious label is that of 'tribe', which has acquired something of a notoriety in the modern world, as tribal societies are sometimes understood by their denigrators to be somehow 'less civilised' than the citizens of states. This is incorrect, and the term simply refers to a form of sociopolitical organisation where clans or lineages of people are grouped together, usually under some form of paramount leader (a 'sheikh'). Anthropological studies of modern tribal societies are useful for conceptualising older ones, who are of course no longer around to be observed and studied. While nobody would suggest that ancient tribes are exactly like modern ones, and vice-versa, the analyses of modern tribes are tremendously helpful in interpreting the relations between Arabs and the Roman Empire. For example, we know that tribal leadership places a premium on skill at negotiation, mediation, and solving disputes. While such activities are usually concerned with the problems within the tribe, when tribes become involved with states, tribal leaders become mediators not just between tribe and state – discussing the swapping of resources between the two, for example – but also within the state itself. Where opportunities could be found in the state which matched the skills and ambitions of a tribal leader, a successful career spanning the conceptual gulf between tribe and state could result. A good example of this phenomenon comes from our period, where the pro-Roman Arab leader Alamoundaros (in power between 569-582) enjoyed a prosperous career out of mediating in the religious disputes within the Roman Empire (we will take a look at Alamoundaros below).

Anthropological studies are important for other reasons, too, because they help to shed new light on situations which can, at first glance, appear very one-sided. For example, while Alamoundaros appears to be simply a loyal servant of the Roman Empire, called in to do the Emperor's bidding as mediator, he was also, in fact, carrying on his traditional conciliatory duties as a tribal sheikh. This is tremendously important, because tribal leaders gained prestige and standing from success in their endeavours, of which mediation was one of the most fruitful. It is also important because it is easy to look at the relationship between Emperor and tribal sheikh and miss the fact that from the perspective of the sheikh, the relationship was probably interpreted as more equal than from the perspective of the Emperor! So while Alamoundaros undeniably helped the Roman Empire by mediating in its religious disputes, he was also, from another perspective, using the Roman Empire to further his own position. State-tribe relations, far from being one-sided, were dynamic, and frequently accrued great benefits to the tribe as well as to the Empire, which gained military manpower and peace along the frontiers, for example.

Similarly, while the Romans typically viewed their allies (whether Arabs or others) as subordinates, the long involvement of Rome in wars against the Sasanian Empire provided a myriad of opportunities for the Arab tribes involved to play Rome and Iran against each other. This is a modern phenomenon too, as mentioned above for the relationship between the British, French, and Native Americans in colonial-period North America; but there are also many more modern examples, such as the relationship between the Rwala bedouin and the Jordanian and Syrian governments. So, again, what looks from the outside to be a subordinated group of allies doing imperial bidding turns out, instead, to be something far more three-dimensional and dynamic. We will see examples of all of this in this book.

Empires and Arabs before the fourth century

As Rome and the Sasanians looked for frontier allies of every kind to escape the growing stalemate in Mesopotamia, Arabs, who were the natural choice along the southern peripheries of both states, were very gradually incorporated into a system of Roman and Sasanian alliances. The fact that both empires had a long tradition of employing 'barbarians' as militia meant that there was nothing particularly novel about this process, and the Arabs were easily slotted in to the template of what is usually called 'clientship.' The Romans, for example, had long used Goths, Vandals, Franks, and others along the Rhine and Danube as militia, swapping military service for perks such as subsidies and settlement rights. These arrangements often began with Roman diplomatic activity in frontier regions, the formation of friendly ties and the establishment of good relations. It seems that very much the same sort of thing was happening in Arabia. Before Arabs ended up as Roman militia, the Romans began with diplomacy.

After the Romans annexed the kingdom of Nabataea in 105/6, they assumed control over parts of the trade route that ran from the spice- and incense-rich regions of southern Arabia – essentially modern Yemen – up the west side of the Arabian Peninsula, and into southern Jordan. At a site on one part of this route, Ruwwafa, now in northwestern Saudi Arabia, a temple was discovered in the twentieth century which contained a bilingual inscription written into the stone in Greek, but also in the form of Aramaic used by many inhabitants of the area (the main part of the inscription from the temple is now in the Riyadh Museum). It is not the most overwhelming of sites to visit, although the surrounding landscape is spectacular, and shattered parts of other inscriptions lie cast around the temple. The main inscription recognised the primacy of the Roman Emperor Marcus Aurelius, and his co-emperor,

Lucius Verus, thus dating the structure to sometime between 161 and 169 (when Verus died). It recorded the dedication of the temple by a group of people called Thamud. This name is known in the lexicon of Arab tribes in the area, and it is possible that the dedicants were acting as allies of the Roman military in the region. For a long while, this was the only evidence of Roman diplomatic or military presence in the area. In 2005, however, the Franco-Saudi mission working at the Nabataean site of Madain Salih, not far from Ruwwafa, made a startling discovery. (Madain Salih is famous for its rock-cut tombs, which were built by the Nabataeans, the same people who constructed Petra). At Madain Salih an inscription was found, which recorded, in Latin, the presence of Roman military officers at the city. Like that of Ruwwafa, this one was also dated to the reign of Marcus Aurelius. It is always a tricky prospect to draw conclusions from inscriptions, which are often short, damaged, or incomplete. Yet what these two examples can be reasonably held to show is that despite the fact that there is little evidence for any major Roman interest in the Arabian Peninsula after the rule of Augustus (d. 14), who had sent an ambitious military expedition to Yemen, by the time of

Marcus Aurelius, the Romans were again making their influence felt in the region. This was the beginning of a process that would eventually lead to formal treaties and Arabs fighting alongside Roman legionaries against their shared Sasanian enemies.

Another piece of evidence from a later period also hints at the development of ties between Romans and Arabs. If you travel to Paris and visit the near eastern antiquities section at the Louvre, you will find, mounted on the wall, a slab of rock with a faint crack running diagonally down the centre. This is the famous inscription from Nemara, a Roman outpost in southern Syria, near the modern Jordanian border. The inscription, dated to 328, during the reign of Constantine, has caused a lot of grief to modern scholars because of its first line:

> '…this is the monument of Imru al-Qays, king of all the Arabs…'

At least that is what it appears to say; but to return to the problem of labels and markers of 'groups' or 'identity', does this mean the Arabs as a 'people'? Even with the caveat that the word 'Arab' is hard to pin down to a single definition, it is an undeniably attractive proposition! (It is not at all clear, and, to give just one example, the line could read 'king of all of arab', which may refer to a region in northern Mesopotamia of the same name.) But expectations are further raised by the fact that this is one of the very first inscriptions to appear in the Arabic language, proving that it was used by the Arabs before the emergence of Islam. Some have taken this as a signal that Imru al-Qays was making a statement about his identity – in other words, that one might say something in a particular language because that language is important to your nation or ethnic group to which you belong. This may be so, and it *cannot* be ruled out that this was the case. But it is also true that linguistic nationalism is a modern phenomenon, and ancient people had much more flexible notions about what the language they spoke said about them.

Interestingly, the inscription is in the Arabic *language*, but it is written using the Aramaic *script* common throughout the region. This is a little like writing out a sentence in English, but using the Cyrillic script from Russia or the Greek script used in Greece to write out the message. So what it tells us (in conjunction with other evidence) is that Arabic was, at the moment, an oral language, one that was mostly spoken, and only rarely written down. It would be some time before the Arabic script developed to become what we know today, and when it did, as discussed above, it happened within the Roman Empire (and more on this in Ch. 5).

So what, if anything, can be said about this inscription? We can state what it isn't – it is not an announcement of ethnic identity, declaring the presence of the Arabs as a people in the modern sense. But there is some hope! Language and identity problems aside, the Nemara inscription is extremely interesting because of what it goes on to say. Imru al-Qays boasts about the peoples he has defeated, providing a catalogue of identifiable tribes ranging throughout the Arabian Peninsula. He says that he carried out some of his expeditions as an Iranian vassal, but also as a Roman one. This suggests that both empires had engaged his services, at some point, to fight their enemies. Again, this was a fairly common ancient practice and it is entirely in keeping with the times. Presumably this information was included on the inscription as the support of Rome and Iran only served to further Imru al-Qays' prestige. The inscription may not give us the means to talk of an Arab people or some kind of ethnic identity, but it does clearly show the presence of Arab leaders who were using alliances with the two ancient superpowers to enlarge their own authority, which is precisely the pattern that follows in the fifth and sixth centuries. The form of the inscription, a so-called *tabula ansata* common in the Roman world, is also an indication of this imperially-inspired link. It was also rather gutsy of the heirs of Imru al-Qays to erect the inscription at the Roman military camp of Nemara. So, the Nemara inscription does seem to be making some kind of a statement about the confidence and political authority of Imru al-Qays, but not necessarily about the 'Arabs' as a whole.

These three examples – Ruwwafa, Madain Salih, and Nemara – indicate, albeit in a very fragmentary form, that the Romans (and Iranians, in the case of Nemara) were interested in cultivating relationships with the peoples who lived south of the Syrian deserts, away from the Euphrates River and the cities and villages of the Fertile Crescent. We can add to this list as well a long inscription found at Paikuli in Kurdistan, which lists a certain Amr of the tribe of

Lakhm as a Sasanian vassal, dated to about 293. Little is heard of this family in contemporary sources until about 500, when they re-emerge as Sasanian allies living at a place called al-Hirah, near the site of modern Baghdad. The picture is thus one of tentative alliances and transfrontier links which appear and then disappear, all pieced together from a tantalisingly brief range of evidence. Neither the Romans nor the Sasanians garrisoned the desert, but their influence was felt well beyond the space where their fortifications stood and their armed patrols ventured. Finally, it is important to keep in mind that while the Romans and Sasanians gained military support from these efforts, as the Nemara inscription shows, they were not one-sided affairs. The Arabs – as Imru al-Qays showed us – gained prestige from association with such powerful states. Eventually, this prestige would be translated into financial and political power, which endowed Arab leaders with leadership of civic and religious communities. This would be crucial for the transition between Roman and Arab hegemony in the Near East.

2

Arabs, Empires, Christianity, and new alliances, 370-528

Roman authors looked on barbarians with disdain. The Roman military officer and historian Ammianus Marcellinus, writing in the late fourth century, claimed that the Arabs were ignorant of vines and cereals, and abandoned themselves to unbridled lust. The full passage is worth quoting:

Yet the Saracens, desired by us neither as friends nor enemies, roaming in different directions here and there, would lay waste to whatever could be found in a short amount of time, like grasping kites, who, if they considered prey at a greater height, seize by a swift flight, and if they succeeded, did not delay. Although I remember having reported upon the customs of those men in the deeds of the Emperor Marcus and several times afterwards, yet now I will likewise report on particulars about the same men intermittently. Among these peoples, the origin of whom commencing from the Assyrians, is extended to the waterfalls of the Nile, and the borders of the Blemmyae, all are warriors by equal lot, half-naked, clothed in coloured cloaks down to the loins, moving slowly through diverse places with the aid of agile horses and thin camels, through tranquil and turbid events; and none of them ever seizes a plough-handle or tends to a tree, or seeks nourishment by conquering arable land, but they always wander through spread out regions wide and far, without a home and without fixed settlements or laws; and they do not long bear the same sky, nor does the sun of one region please them. Their life is always in flight, and their wives are mercenaries, hired for a time from a contract, and (so that they may be a matrimonial species) the future wife offers to her husband a spear and a tent in the name of a dowry, to depart after the set time (if she chooses that), and it is unbelievable the intensity with which each sex among them is released into intercourse. Yet they wander widely thus as long as they live, so that a woman may marry in one place, give birth in another place, and rear children far away, allowed no opportunity of resting. All their nourishment is game meat, and an abundant supply of milk, by which they are sustained, and numerous herbs, and, if they are able, such birds to be captured through bird-catching, and we have seen most of them thoroughly unaware of the enjoyment of grain and wine. Enough about this destructive people (translated by Anik Laferriere).

This sort of characterisation was common in Roman representations of all kinds of barbarians. Ammianus, who wrote a sober and often reliable history of the time, mentioned that the Huns used to eat meat which they had placed between their thighs and their horses to warm up slightly (although I am reliably told by one of my students that this *does* tenderise the meat – creating a form of tartare!).

Literary perceptions of barbarians, including Arabs, altered when the Roman Empire formally became a Christian state in the fourth century. Barbarians were still uncivilised, of course, and deserved to be castigated as such in the eyes of Roman observers, but they also represented potential converts. In short, if barbarians would convert, they might be able to join the universal Christian community represented by the Christian Roman Empire, in which the Roman Emperor sat in Constantinople as God's viceroy. Whereas they had previously been uncivilised and damned, now barbarians might be saved – if only they would recognise the error of their pagan ways. This outlook had a dramatic impact, because it meant that no matter the origin of a particular barbarian, he could at least find a façade of 'Romanness' by being Christian. Christian writers express precisely this sort of view, often in the same breath as damning Arabs for raiding, theft, and all kinds of other misdeeds. But the literary rhetoric concealed an important truth of the new Roman Empire, which was that converts could, and did, join the political ranks of the Empire as bishops, priests, military officers, and scholars. Of course, if Arabs remained pagan, then all bets were off; Roman authors took glee in highlighting the execrable activities of 'heathen' Arabs, who sacrificed children, worshipped what the Romans saw as false gods, and all manner of other terrible things. St. Jerome, for example, wrote with evident glee in his biography of St. Malchus about the latter's capture by Arabs, who forced him to go naked and tend to the flocks (i.e., the opposite of a settled, clothed, civilised existence). This was all part of the rhetoric of late Roman literature, a great deal of which had an unmistakeable Christian bias. St. Jerome's story entertained, as well as moralised: his audience would have found the story instructive, as well as highly amusing, and there were many like it doing the rounds in late antiquity.

The consequences of all of this for the Arabs are not difficult to imagine, and in fact it would not be understating the fact to assert that, without the cultural glue afforded by Christianity, a pre-eminent Arab family known as the Jafnids, who were allies of the Romans in the sixth century, would likely not have achieved the position that they did (we shall return to the Jafnids below, in Chapter 3). In other words, only those who became Christian could expect to reach high levels of power in the late Roman world. (There are exceptions, of course, but these generally serve to prove the rule.) Thus it is that stories abound about Arabs adopting Christianity, as well as those of Arab military alliances infused with Christian symbolism and overtones. For example, a number of Christian authors – Sozomen, Theodoret, Rufinus, and Socrates Scholasticus – picked up a story about an Arab queen called Mavia, active at around the end of the fourth century. Mavia's husband had held a treaty of alliance with the Roman Emperor Valens, who followed an interpretation of Christianity called Arianism. Arianism had been deemed heretical at the Council of Nicaea in 325, but it remained popular for some time afterwards, even if continually demonised. Notably, the Arian Valens died a fiery death in battle at Adrianople in 378, which was seen by some on the 'orthodox' side as just retribution! But before that event, Valens broke the treaty which had been held with Mavia's husband - a normal practice, in fact, since most treaties were made between individuals, not between states or groups. Even treaties between Rome and the Sasanians usually needed renegotiating when one party died. Yet Mavia refused to negotiate, offended, it seems, by Valens' Arian Christianity. We might be suspicious here since the stories of the episode usually appear in anti-Arian contexts, but whatever the case, Mavia launched a vicious rebellion in which she defeated in battle the most senior Roman military commander in the east. Eventually a halt was called when Valens assented to her demand for a bishop of her choosing, which she duly received, and Mavia cemented the arrangement by marrying her daughter off to a Roman officer, Victor. All was forgiven – so much so that after Valens was killed in 378 by a Gothic army at Adrianople and Constantinople itself threatened, Mavia's forces sprang to the rescue. In his account of the event, the historian Ammianus (a pagan, not a Christian) spoke of the terror which Mavia and her Arabs instilled in the Goths. The story as a whole is remarkable not just as a good piece of ecclesiastical entertainment, but also because it indicates, even in a slightly hyperbolic fashion, an essential truth of Roman frontier arrangements: Christianity was a powerful tool with which to bind non-Roman and Roman together, and peace in religious relations was essential for those frontier arrangements to work. If two incompatible types of Christians – Arians and orthodox, for example – tried to work together, the result might be a rebellion, or worse. But beyond these divisions, Arabs, as much as any other barbarian people, were seen as (more) trustworthy by the Romans when they adopted Christianity. Of course, assessing issues such as devotion is impossible, and largely a waste of time: appearances were usually much more important.

Other stories illustrate what could be achieved by Arabs when they became Christian. In the early fifth century an adventurer and émigré from the Sasanian Empire arrived in Palestine to see St. Euthymius, a local hermit. The adventurer's name was Aspebetos (the name, John Trimingham suggests, is a corruption of a Sasanian military position, *spahbedh*) and he brought with him his son, Terebon. The young boy had an illness which the Zoroastrian priests in the Sasanian Empire could not cure, and coupled with the evident disquiet that Aspebetos reported upon seeing Christians persecuted in Iran (again, we should not necessarily believe the rhetoric deployed here by the author of the story), Aspebetos was ready and primed for conversion. Sure enough, when he did adopt Christianity, his son was healed by St. Euthymius, and a little while afterwards, his people were converted as well. The story, told by Cyril of Scythopolis, a biographer of saints and holy men, includes a range of common devices used to emphasise the finality and correctness of conversion. By becoming Christian, for example, Aspebetos and his people went from being slaves to being free; they gave up being 'wolves of Arabia', in Cyril's words, and instead became 'rational'; and so on. Ideas of a *turn* away from old to new were popularised in the conversion story of St. Augustine in the *Confessions,* and were familiar parts of conversion stories. The biblical idea of a sick person who could only be healed by taking the faith and being baptised was also extremely common in late antiquity, and frequently used to show how Arabs and other barbarians came to adopt the faith. Other examples of this sort of story are found in the biographies of St. Symeon the Stylite, a saint who lived on a pillar in Syria. On numerous occasions St. Symeon healed paralysed Arabs, made fertile the infertile, and performed other miracles. Another example comes from a story appended to that of Mavia, told by the church historian Sozomen. A certain Zokomos sought out baptism so that he might have a son. Baptism was succeeded instantaneously and miraculously by a trouble-free birth. The story of Aspebetos and Terebon is thus a nice example of how Christian authors imagined Arabs were converted, while that and the other stories discussed here show how Roman Christian writers explained how Arabs might gain what they interpreted as 'true' Christian civilisation.

With Aspebetos, though, we have an additional piece of evidence, which confirms that while many of the stories might be rhetorical or moralising in purpose, it *was* true that people could gain access to remarkable opportunities by joining the Roman Christian commonwealth. Upon baptism, Cyril of Scythopolis tells us that Aspebetos changed his name to Peter and became a bishop, attending the famous Council of Ephesus in 431. This was one of the many meetings convened under the auspices of the Roman state, to debate and decide on orthodoxy and heresy. We know that Peter was real and indeed attended, because his name appears in the subscriptions from the council. There, he is recorded as 'Peter, bishop of the Parembole', referring to the name of the camp established for him and his followers.

A little later, another adventurer and refugee from the Sasanian Empire arrived in southern Jordan. This man was called Amorkesos, which is one way to write, in Greek, the name Imru al-Qays (no relation to he of the Nemara inscription). Amorkesos seized upon a moment of Roman military weakness: a large expedition sent by the emperor Leo to North Africa had just foundered off Cape Bon, Tunisia, a victim of betrayal by a bankrupt Roman general. Much of the Roman army vanished with the expedition, compounding the losses from Adrianople nearly a century earlier, which had proved hard to replace. Facing denuded defences, Amorkesos defeated the local Roman forces and took for himself an island called Iotabe, which has yet to be identified, but is thought to be in the Gulf of Aqaba. This was a customs post that taxed the trade flowing out of southern Arabia into the Roman Empire, and now Amorkesos took this income for himself. Quickly realising, however, that these funds were likely to be missed by their intended recipients in the imperial palace, he scraped together a diplomatic mission to Constantinople, and dressed up his position by bringing with him a priest. The story is told by a writer named Malchus, who hated Leo (he calls him 'Leo the Butcher') and who looks sourly on Leo's decision to receive Amorkesos, a barbarian, in the imperial capital. But there, Leo showered the Arab with gold and gifts and invited him to supper with the local aristocracy. Leo took Amorkesos' 'Christianity' with a pinch of salt – it seems clear that he knew Amorkesos was pretending – but allowed him to hang on to Iotabe. This might be because the Romans were still too weak to mount an offensive to take it back. Such an offensive did happen, but only much later on, under the Emperor Anastasius (r. 491-518). But like the story of Mavia, that of Amorkesos reveals the important role of a shared Christian religion in creating ties of trust and obligation, even when it was an open secret that religious devotion had been manufactured purely for the sake of appearances. Amorkesos could be accepted as a rogue who had illegally stolen imperial property, because he, and the Emperor, had something in common.

Why was Christianity attractive to Arabs? Again, it is not necessary to look for issues of devotion or theology, although doubtless these played a role for some, as they have done for religious converts since the beginning of time. The ancient world had a complex matrix of deities who fulfilled a wide range of functions. Well before the dominance of monotheistic religions, it was common to seek out different gods to address issues of fertility, rain, disease, and so on. During the Republic, the Romans had subsumed a range of 'foreign' gods into their pantheon during times of crisis, such as in the Second Punic War, fought against Hannibal of Carthage between 218-201 BC. And even when the Empire took Christianity as the state religion, other beliefs did not vanish, nor was there (yet) a concerted state-wide effort to eradicate them. For many, then, the powers of the Christian God could simply be 'added' to one's own pantheon, an idea underscored by the propensity of healing stories. In a world with primitive medical care, divine healing was always useful. But there were other factors at play, too. One feature of late antique religious life was the movement of hundreds of holy men and women into the deserts to pursue the life of hermits. It was these people whom Arabs encountered as they traded with Roman villagers, migrated from drought, or sought military service with the Roman army. Then, far more than now, holy men and women held great prestige, and when this was coupled with political authority via connection to the officially-sanctioned state religion, or the ability to heal and protect, it is not difficult to see how conversion might easily follow. There are numerous stories of holy men arbitrating tribal quarrels in the manner of tribal leaders, and it seems that at least in some cases the prestige of holy men was held to be equivalent to that of a tribal sheikh. Holy men and women were also mediators – between heaven and earth, desert and village, and so on, and this mediatory capacity also mimicked the way that tribal sheikhs dealt with their followers. Finally, some monks and bishops went out of their way to attract Arab converts. In the manner of colonial European missionaries learning the language and customs of those they wished to convert, late antique holy men made it possible for the eucharist to be celebrated away from the altar (i.e., on the move, suitable for people who may have been nomads, some of the time); they named churches after individual tribes; and by going to the Arabs, rather than the other way around, they made it easy for their message to be internalised and appropriated.

By the end of the fifth century, large numbers of Arabs living along the edges of the Roman Empire had become Christian. Further to the south, into the Arabian Peninsula, the religious map is much less clear because of problems with the source material. There certainly were Christians in Arabia, as religions tensions between

Jews and Christians were a characteristic of sixth-century life in the region of Najran, now in Saudi Arabia, and there are records of a church being built in San'a, in Yemen. Recent work on the populations of the Arabian Peninsula, including the kingdom of Himyar, in modern Yemen, confirms the presence of Jewish populations as well.

The best evidence for Arab Christianity comes from the sixth century, with the Jafnid family, who assumed an important role in late Roman church politics after 528. After turning to examine political and military developments between 378 and 528, we will come back to the Jafnids and their arch-rivals, the Nasrids, who, under their formidable leader al-Mundhir III, were the favoured Arab allies of the Sasanians.

3

Political and military affairs on the frontier, 378-528

As noted above in Chapter 1, the Ruwwafa inscription from Saudi Arabia suggests that Arabs had been involved as early as 161-169 (or thereabouts) in some sort of military arrangement with the Roman army. The specifics are not clear, and the lack of details on the inscriptions from Paikuli in Kurdistan, and Nemara in Syria, also mean that understanding the details of any treaty arrangements can present a challenge. This situation changes after 378, when Mavia's forces helped to defend Constantinople against the Goths. By 528, when the Jafnid family came to power, the Empire had created a web of alliances which protected the eastern and southern areas of the Roman state. Over to the east, the Sasanians had also developed an alliance with a family known as the Nasrids, descendants of the Amr who appears on the inscription in Kurdistan. All of this makes sense in light of the changing nature of the conflict between Rome and the Sasanians during this period, and by the introduction of a new and powerful actor, the kingdom of Himyar in southern Arabia, which came to prominence after 275.

A unique document, the *Notitia Dignitatum*, known from a medieval manuscript, records the dispositions of the military units of the Roman Empire in about 420. The list itemises the various forts and other bases, provides illustrations of shield insignia, and informs on a wide range of other fascinating information. Several of the hundreds of military units recorded in the *Notitia* are designated *Saraceni*; this indicates that they were drawn from Arabs, since by the late fourth century, Roman authors had started using the term *Saracen* to refer to the Arabs of the desert. The name was used, for example, by Ammianus Marcellinus to refer to the so-called *scenitai* or 'tent-dwellers', and differentiated them from those 'civilised' Arabs who might live in cities or villages. The appearance of *Saraceni* in the 420s is consonant with Roman attempts throughout the Empire to push beyond the villages of the frontier areas to find and enrol barbarians in the military. In the west, for example, Goths, Alans, Franks, Vandals, and other Germans joined the Roman army in large numbers in the fourth and fifth centuries; some achieved high office, like the half-German Stilicho, a prominent warlord in the early part of the fifth century who married into the imperial family.

During the same time period, the Romans were also making more formal arrangements with Arabs whom they preferred not to absorb into the army, but to use as more arms'-length militia. Again, this was a common process in the Empire. In the west, such allies took the name *foederati*, or federates, after the Latin word for treaty, *foedus*. It was understood that federates were political subordinates, even if, as greater numbers of barbarians joined the army, they gained a more equal standing over time. In the east, where Greek was the language of administration and bureaucracy, such federates were called *hupospondoi*, from the Greek word *spondos*, meaning treaty; Malchus, the author who narrates the tale of Amorkesos, mentions in an aside that *hupospondoi* and *foederati* were more or less the same thing in Roman eyes. Since Arabs were usually taken on as militia allies in the east, they tended to be called *hupospondoi*, not *foederati*. There are numerous examples across the range of ancient literature of Arabs employed in this capacity.

Arabs could thus be enrolled into the army, taken on as *hupospondoi*, and they could also fill in a third category. This was the office of *phylarch*, another Greek word, which means 'tribal leader.' This was, in many respects, the most remote-controlled of all the ways that Roman agents attempted to bring Arabs into Roman service, because *phylarchs*, who tended to be the chiefs of individual tribes, worked closely with Roman regional military commanders but did not necessarily have access to any other office. An Arab *phylarch* in the fifth century could not realistically go on and be a military commander of a Roman unit, for example, without leaving his position. The system of *phylarchates* seems to have spread across the frontier provinces of the Roman East, including Syria, Phoenicia, Arabia, and so on, and was primarily intended to provide extra muscle to Roman commanders on the ground. There are numerous examples of Arab *phylarchs* taking part in campaigns against the Sasanians, doing local protection and policing work, putting down revolts, and so on. They fit the job description of ad-hoc militia quite well and held the added attraction for the Romans of helping to keep the *phylarch*-led tribes peaceful. An unruly tribe might cost the *phylarch* his position (and perhaps his liberty or his life as well).

It seems that for much of the fifth century, these different and complementary arrangements worked reasonably well. There were only two brief wars with Iran in 421 and 441 (both, incidentally, linked to religious tensions) and much of the attention of emperors in Constantinople was taken up with other concerns. To the south, though, things were afoot in the Arabian Peninsula that would affect the nature and functioning of the Roman alliance system along the southern frontiers of the Empire.

The kingdom of Himyar and the Arabian Peninsula

In 275, the kingdom of Himyar, roughly equivalent to part of modern Yemen, annexed the kingdom of Saba (of 'Queen of Sheba' fame). Over the subsequent two hundred years, the Himyarites set about establishing their dominion in central Arabia. Perhaps recognising, as the Romans had done, that rule by remote control was cheaper and often more effective than costly conquest and occupation, the rulers of Himyar seem to have co-opted Arab tribes and used them as proxies. The history of how all this happened has been reconstructed in detail through the work of the French scholar Christian Robin and his research team in Paris, and is largely based on a small corpus of inscriptions found scattered throughout modern Saudi Arabia, and a sparse range of literary texts. A bibliography of Professor Robin's publications is provided at the end of this book.

An undated inscription found near the modern Saudi capital of Riyadh describes an expedition by the Himyarites to a place called 'the land of Ma'add.' This is usually understood to be the area to the north of Riyadh, lying in a wedge between the lower parts of the Roman and Sasanian empires. Later Muslim traditions talk of a man named Hujr, son of Amr, taking control of Ma'add, and it is possible that the expedition that appears in the inscription was a Himyarite attempt to install Hujr as their proxy. Hujr also appears on a different inscription as 'king of Kinda', referring to the tribe from which he originated. Kinda also shows up on an inscription dated to 521 describing a Himyarite military campaign into the Sasanian Empire. Hujr may not have been the only proxy ruler for Himyar, as another – a certain Numanan – is also recorded. What does all of this tell us? The Himyarite rulers boasted that they had power over the Arabs of the coast and the highlands; it was they, not the Arabs, who controlled large parts of the peninsula. Despite this, they clearly tolerated their subordinates calling themselves 'kings', but this was probably because the word meant something quite different to them than it does to us, denoting élite status among the tribal milieu rather than any royal pretension.

Himyar's control of the Arabian Peninsula did not present an immediate threat to either the Romans or the Sasanians, despite the attempts of both to build a presence on their respective sides of the peninsula. The Romans had enjoined relations with Axum (Ethiopia), a Christian ally who could be used as a Roman proxy in the region. Trade routes in the Red Sea and along the side of the peninsula made this attractive. The Sasanians were interested in Bahrain and Qatar and other areas nearby. Thus the Romans sought influence in western Arabia, and the Sasanians primarily in the east. But by the end of the fifth century, both superpowers were drawn into northern Arabia, and this brought them into the affairs of the Himyarites. The reason for this is that the descendants of Hujr, who had taken control of Ma'add on Himyar's behalf, were involved in a struggle with the Nasrids, Sasanian Iran's Arab clients based at al-Hirah in Iraq. This struggle, which would see at least one expedition by the family of Hujr, the 'Hujrids', to sack the base of the Nasrids at al-Hirah, was also punctuated by periods of calm when marriage alliances were concluded. In brief, though, these actions brought the Hujrid family and their allies into the sphere of Roman-Sasanian competition, and since Ma'add sat practically at the edge of the broad area of southern Roman influence, this spurred the Romans, particularly, to act.

  At the end of the fifth century, Roman diplomats and agents were active in northern Arabia. We know of their activities from a remarkable text by Nonnosus, a career diplomat whose family was also employed in Roman service. (By an accident of history, his writings about his profession ended up being excerpted by a Byzantine clergyman named Photius – without Photius, we would know much less.) The Romans initiated a diplomatic blitz to woo the Hujrids onto the Roman side, and stem the influence of the Nasrids and thus, by extension, the Sasanians in northern Arabia, a region from which the Roman flank could be threatened. The strategy worked, aided by a timely invasion of Himyar by Rome's ally Axum. The invasion of Himyar probably convinced the Hujrids that they should jump on board with the Romans, whose power in the region was clearly ascendant. It would not perhaps be overly cynical to see Axum's invasion and Roman diplomacy as part of the same whole, and indeed the Roman author Procopius places these two events quite neatly together. It is not clear if, in the process, they abandoned their responsibilities to the Himyarites, but the Hujrids were now Roman allies. It was a strategic triumph for the Roman Emperor Anastasius: with a minimum of expense and effort, he had denied northern Arabia to the Sasanians and obtained a useful ally which could be used to strike into southern Iraq. The alliance continued into the late 520s, at which point Roman diplomats extended their reach to southern Arabia in the wake of the Axumite victory.

Changing times

Though the main arena of competition between the Roman and Sasanian empires remained the chequerboard of fortified cities in Mesopotamia, the stalemate there and changes in the balance of power in northern Arabia, discussed above, had forced the Romans to intensify their search for allies in the deserts of the Arabian Peninsula. As mentioned earlier, the inscription at Ruwwafa indicates that this process had begun as early as the second century, but by the fifth and sixth it was now well-advanced. The Hujrids became *phylarchs* under Anastasius and visited Constantinople, and their alliance protected the southern approaches to the Roman Empire as well as the flank of the spice route – the western strip of the Arabian Peninsula, linking the spice-producing areas of Yemen to Roman markets in the Middle East and further afield. This was not an easily-fortified area, nor one where armies could travel freely; it was a sound policy to seek allies familiar with the territory to control it. Relations with Himyar continued to be a factor, especially after Axumite control of the kingdom waned. Religious tensions between Christians and Jews in the 520s triggered a famous event at Najran, where it is usually held that a large number of Christians were killed under the auspices of the Jewish Himyarite king, Dhu Nuwas (the kings of Himyar appear to have converted to Judaism in the fourth century). Religious strife was common and, unsurprisingly, this event looms large in Christian texts and spawned numerous stories told of the 'martyrs of Najran.' It is, however, best understood as part of the wider picture: striking at Christians also constituted a strike against Rome and her hated Axumite ally, and, indeed, the events at Najran were part of a revolt against Axumite rule. Dhu Nuwas, casting around for allies, is said to have sent a messenger to the pagan Nasrid ruler at al-Hirah, al-Mundhir III, inviting him to join in a persecution against Christians there. In a period where interstate relations were rarely, if ever, disassociated from religious concerns, religious violence and persecution formed a regular and familiar part of political and military campaigns.

The developments described here thus mandated, for the Romans, a great interest in the Arabian Peninsula. This was necessary to protect Roman trading interests and, as much as possible, Christian communities at the fringes of imperial control, for whom the commonwealth felt a profound obligation. 'Protecting Christians' outside the Empire could also be a useful pretext for war. It was also necessary to deny allies to the Sasanians (it is not clear if the Hujrids were Christianised, but it would not be a surprise if this was the case) and to prevent the Sasanians from gaining any sort of advantage which might disrupt Roman power in the area. The Arabian Peninsula rarely, if ever, features in Roman history textbooks, but it was a crucial part of the Roman political, diplomatic, religious, and military picture in late antiquity. It is worth keeping in mind that the Romans had extensive experience at projecting power through diplomacy, proxies, and allies, and that many areas, such as Arabia, were used as the arena for such efforts.

In the end, the alliance with the Hujrids was not sustained, as a new set of circumstances dictated a change. In about 527-528, the leader of the Hujrids, a man called al-Harith, was killed in battle in Syria by al-Mundhir III. This man was rapidly establishing a reputation for himself as a dangerous and unpredictable foe. Following al-Harith's death, the Roman Emperor Justinian – who had taken his throne in the same year – arrived at a novel solution, which was essentially to stop relying on a complex system of *phylarchs*, *hupospondoi*, and others under a kaleidoscope of rulers, and instead to install a single man as the supreme leader of Rome's Arab allies. This man, known as Arethas (the Greek rendering of al-Harith, but not related to the al-Harith mentioned above), together with his son, Alamoundaros, constitute the best-documented Arabs of the pre-Islamic period. We will turn now to look at the career of Arethas and his family, as well as that of the almost-undefeatable al-Mundhir III. Since there are certain amounts of overlap in this story, we will begin in the year 497, shortly before the Hujrid alliance was concluded by Anastasius. And to avoid confusion, we shall leave the name al-Harith behind, and use the Greek term, Arethas, to refer to the Jafnid leader elevated by Justinian in 527/8.

4

New Arab allies, 497-602

The chronicler Theophanes, writing a long time after events, tells us that in 497, there was an invasion of the 'tent-dwelling Arabs' into parts of Syria. By this he meant the Saracens or *scenitai*, the people whom the Romans considered to be nomads – barbarous and uncivilised. Roman officers were equal to the task, and Romanus, the regional commander in Palestine, dealt with the invasions that came his way. During these skirmishes a man named Gabalas had been defeated by Romanus, and the energetic Roman officer followed up on a successful campaigning season by liberating the island of Iotabe from the Arab adventurer Amorkesos, who, as detailed above, had taken in it sometime around 473.

    This was just one of many border wars fought between Roman forces and Arab raiders, but the presence of Gabalas is important, because it was his son, Arethas, and his grandson, Alamoundaros, who would go on to play such an important role as Roman allies under Justinian and his successors. The Arab invasions of 497 could have had any number of causes, but later Muslim Arab historians, such as al-Tabari (writing between 838 and 923) and al-Masudi (896-956) mention drought and population pressures as recurring catalysts for the movements of people north into the 'Fertile Crescent.' It is very likely that such issues lay behind the events of 497, and that it was at this time that part, or all, of the tribe of Ghassan entered the Roman Empire. This event is momentous, since it brought into contact with the Romans the leading clan of Ghassan – the so-called Jafnid family, who would become the pre-eminent Arab allies of the Romans for much of the sixth century. Gabalas is the first known of the Jafnids, and his son, Arethas, and grandson, Alamoundaros, will occupy much of the story as we go forward.

The career of Gabalas is something of a black hole. There are no contemporary sources for his activities, and we do not know if he held a formal alliance, became Christian (although this was expected of Roman allies), or fought any battles on behalf of Rome. Indeed, between 497 and 527, the Romans seem to have maintained their focus on the Hujrids, but they were fighting a losing battle against a new enemy – the energetic, dangerous, and clever al-Mundhir III, who came from the family of Arabs living at al-Hirah in Iraq, allied to the Sasanian Empire since at least 293. By 527, when the Roman Emperor Justinian assumed the throne, a new policy was launched. The contemporary historian Procopius explains that al-Mundhir III plundered and killed almost at will, and that neither the Roman commanders nor the Arab *phylarchs* – presumably the Hujrids and their allies – could stop him. Al-Mundhir took prisoners by the thousands, Procopius says, either killing them outright or ransoming them for vast sums of money. Things got so bad that two senior Roman generals, Timostratus and John, were captured – later, the Romans were forced to swallow their pride, and send an envoy to ransom them. Procopius finishes his account by explaining that al-Mundhir was the most serious of Rome's enemies at the time.

All this seems to have prompted Justinian to abandon the series of fragmented alliances constructed by his predecessors, of which the Hujrids were the most prominent part, and put up as a sort of chief- or super-*phylarch* in the person of Arethas, the son of Gabalas. Presumably this means that Gabalas had held some sort of official position between 497 and 527, in order for his son to have had the opportunity to distinguish himself. From around this time there is an Arabic graffito from Jebel Seis in southern Syria, which describes Arethas as 'malik', the Arabic term for king. Thus it is clear that somehow, by 527, Arethas had obtained some kind of reputation. It should again be kept in mind that the word 'king' here doesn't necessarily hold the same connotations which we would expect it to today – rather, it suggests élite status among the tribe. There is a parallel in the same period in north Africa, where leaders of Berber tribes took the Latin title *rex*, 'king', with similar meanings. In any case, Arethas was of considerable importance in immediate circles, and the treatment that Justinian gave him was unusual enough for Procopius to state that this sort of thing had never been done before. Justinian, Procopius goes on to say, also gave Arethas the 'dignity of king' – a vague and unexplained comment which probably means more titles, and plenty of money. All this happened at the same time as the last Hujrid leader, al-Harith, was killed by al-Mundhir III. The Romans were nearly out of Arab allies, al-Mundhir was ascendant, and Arethas was now on his own: would Justinian's gamble pay off?

To begin with, the answer seemed to be no: the raids of al-Mundhir continued unabated, and things went from bad to worse at the battle of Callinicum in 531, when the Romans were roundly defeated by their Sasanian adversaries. It did not help that the Roman forces were fasting for Easter, and went to battle on an empty stomach; nonetheless, Procopius blamed Arethas squarely for the defeat and even accused him of cowardice. This may simply be scapegoating, as barbarians were always easy targets. Later, Arethas would also be accused by Procopius of lying to Roman officers so that he could get extra plunder, and of carrying on his own missions without permission. There is some evidence to suggest that while the Romans looked on the Arabs as subordinates, the Arab leaders interpreted their relationship with the state somewhat differently – in more equal terms, and in terms of the opportunities that they could wring out of them. Arethas, then, would not have been 'lying' or deceiving Roman commanders – simply acting in the way he thought most appropriate for his position.

Arethas was the leader of the Jafnid family until 568. While he campaigned for the Romans on numerous occasions, he is best known for his political acumen and his involvement in the religious affairs of the Roman Empire. In the first instance, he built a diplomatic portfolio for the Jafnids that saw something quite extraordinary: Jafnid envoys, alongside Roman ones, representing Arab interests on an embassy to king Abraha of Himyar in 548. The information for this comes from a long inscription on a dam at Marib in Yemen.

In religious affairs, Arethas emerged as a supporter of the Christian doctrine of monophysitism. Monophysitism was an interpretation of Christianity which stressed the 'single nature' of Christ (the Greek compound word of *mono-* and *physis* means 'one spirit' or 'one nature') and it differed subtly from the 'Chalcedonian' interpretation of Christianity that was supported and promoted by the Roman Empire. After the adoption of Christianity by the Roman Empire, which took place in the beginning of the fourth century under Constantine, a significant part of the job of the Roman Emperor became to oversee the development and maintenance of orthodox belief. Rulings on what was acceptable were delivered at church councils, such as the famous Council of Chalcedon in 451. There, heresies were anathematised and the Empire promoted its own brand of Christianity. After 451, the so-called 'Chalcedonian' orthodox interpretation of Christianity would become the dominant form, while the monophysite or 'Jacobite' church would split off from the Chalcedonians permanently. But all of that was a long way off, and in the middle of the sixth century, the waters were very muddy indeed. It was perfectly possible, while debates over exactly what was 'the right sort' of Christianity continued, to support the monophysites, especially since throughout the sixth century Roman emperors repeatedly attempted to find a solution that would allow the monophysites to become full members of Roman religious life. But aside from any personal conviction he may have held (and which is impossible to measure), becoming a supporter of the monophysites gave Arethas a very promising political opportunity, for monophysitism was quite popular in the rural areas of Syria and Arabia where we know that the Jafnids were active. It was, in short, an opportunity to build a power base, tied to an interpretation of the state religion that was at arms'-length from the Emperor and the state itself, without being entirely deemed heretical. It was a perfect middle ground, and a way to become Roman without becoming *too* Roman. And it gave Arethas – and his son – incredible political clout in the imperial capital. While Roman emperors did persecute monophysites from time to time, the prospect of religious disunity was also a very serious matter of internal security and stability, and often of greater concern than fighting the Sasanians. Imperial unity had to come first, and so emperors repeatedly tried to find ways to settle affairs with the monophysites by negotiation. Having a trusted ally who also had the confidence of the monophysites was thus a valuable tool for the Emperor, and this gave Arethas credibility in both camps.

The Arab leader's great coup came in 542. Before the accession of Justinian in 527, a period of persecution had cost the monophysites a large proportion of their bishops. Arethas quickly grasped the opportunity presented to him, and, using his personal connection to the Emperor – it was, after all, Justinian who had personally elevated him – he gained the support of Justinian's wife, Theodora, who harboured monophysite sympathies. The result was two new bishops for the beleaguered monophysites: Jacob Baradeus, who would eventually give his name to the 'Jacobites', and Theodore, who was nominally installed at Bostra, now in southern Syria. These two now set out to consecrate a new range of clergy and begin the process of building up a monophysite ecclesiastical hierarchy.

So what had Arethas gained? Firstly, he had, through his actions, and perhaps almost by accident, become the patron and benefactor of the whole monophysite population in the Roman east. That this conferred power and respect is clear. But now he was also associated with Jacob, who rapidly became the senior member of the monophysites. This link to a revered holy man thus enlarged his prestige further, while the fact that the imperial establishment lay behind Jacob's appointment prevented any of this being perceived as a threat to the Emperor's right to control of religious affairs. It was a diplomatic masterstroke of the highest order – and it catapulted Arethas into the ranks of the Roman élite. He now assumed the prestige title of *patrikios*, which referred to the old Republican patrician order, the wealthiest and most influential members of Roman society. It may have been largely honorific, but we know that the respect that he and his family gained went far beyond simple titles.

A manuscript (*BL* Add. 14602) furnishes some of the proof. It is a collection of correspondence, written in Syriac, a form of Aramaic used in ecclesiastical circles. Traces of the Jafnid family's activities are scattered throughout, including a letter between Arethas and Jacob Baradeus. In another letter Arethas takes the title 'Christ-loving and glorious *patrikios*', and is involved in mediating in the religious dispute between monophysites and the so-called Tritheists (another heretical position of the time) around which much of the *BL* manuscript focuses. Arethas' son Alamoundaros also appears, identified through the subscription of a clergyman, Mar Eustathios, who calls himself presbyter of 'the church of the glorious and Christ-loving *patrikios*, Alamoundaros.'

Mediation and involvement in church-building (rather than church-organisation) was just part of the picture, for Arethas, and then his son, also capitalised on their religious position to assume a high-profile connection to a famous martyr cult, the cult of St. Sergius. Here the muddy waters also helped the Jafnids, because the Sergius cult was open to both monophysites and Chalcedonians, and backing it gave Arethas and his son more clout in Jordan and Syria where the cult was very popular. At Nitl, in Jordan, there is a church south of the famous site of Mt. Nebo, where Moses is reputed to have been buried, and that was excavated in the late twentieth century. Mosaic inscriptions there show that the church was dedicated to the cult of St. Sergius, and some of the same inscriptions mention, in Greek, the names of prominent members of the Jafnid family. During the same period, Arethas also patronised monasteries in Syria and his brother, Abu-Karib, appears as 'king' on a manuscript found at a separate monastery near the ancient site of Palmyra. The picture is thus one of Christian patronage, not just of the Sergius cult, but of Christian populations in the wider area. Arethas' son, Alamoundaros, continued what his father had started. In 2009, engineers in Jordan working on road improvements to Queen Alia International Airport uncovered another church, very close to the one at Nitl, which contained a long Greek inscription in the apse. It identified the church as another dedicated to the Sergius cult, and called for the protection of Alamoundaros, associated here as well with the senior Roman military rank of *comes*, or 'count.'

Alamoundaros also appears, again, always with Greek inscriptions, on buildings scattered throughout Jordan and Syria, either as a benefactor or in an honorific capacity. The most important piece of evidence though is from the fortress city of Resafa, also known as Sergiopolis, in northern Syria, which was the home of the cult of Sergius in the Roman Empire.

Resafa is a large and well-fortified site about a day's march south of the Euphrates in northern Syria. Inside, the cult was venerated in a large basilica, on to which a mosque was added by the Muslim caliph Hisham after the Muslim conquest of Syria. Resafa contains numerous other churches and is also famous for its beautiful and ornate northern gateway, which led pilgrims into the city and to the celebration of the cult. Outside the city is a rather odd square building whose plan mimics the Sergius basilica inside, and in the 'apse' of this building, a Greek inscription records that 'the fortune of Alamoundaros triumphs.'

This style of inscription is clichéd to the point of being worn and hackneyed, and its essential style is found elsewhere in the late Roman Empire. What was this building for? The site of Resafa, which has been extensively excavated by German archaeologists and also written about in detail by Elizabeth Key Fowden, was a natural crossroads, and the cult would have brought additional traffic through the city. Much of this traffic would have included Arabs, amongst whom the Sergius cult seems to have been very popular. It is probable that the so-called 'Al-Mundhir building' was a place where the Jafnid leader could meet his people and engage in the traditional chiefly jobs of negotiation, mediation, and the kind of face-to-face leadership very common amongst late Roman barbarian societies. What it also offered was a way for Alamoundaros to associate himself with all the power of the Roman Empire while sitting, physically, *outside* the walls of the Roman fortress nearby. Like his father, he had found a way to become Roman without being *too* Roman. It was clever – and it bolstered his power.

Like Arethas, Alamoundaros also fought Rome's battles as a militia commander. We know very little about what sort of army he led, and it is entirely possible that it included Romans as well as Arabs. In the 570s and 580s, there were numerous wars with the Sasanians which reflect the growing importance of Arab allies in bolstering the armies of both states. Indeed, it was not long before that the two empires had signed a treaty that officially mandated that the Arab allies of both would be forbidden from attacking each other and would have to adhere to the general terms of the treaty. The technical Greek language of this treaty, recorded by the historian Menander the Guardsman, is of great interest, because it is written in the language of equal alliance, not of *hupospondoi* and *foederati*. It seems to reflect a realisation amongst both Roman and Sasanian diplomats that the Arabs were of much greater import militarily and politically than before – something which, ironically, neither empire would really pay attention to when it mattered, in the mid-seventh century.

By this time, the dangerous al-Mundhir III, the Sasanian Nasrid ally, was dead. He had been killed in battle by Arethas in 554, and now the Nasrids put up a string of weak and ineffectual leaders against whom Arethas' son, Alamoundaros, succeeded with ease. He sacked the Nasrid city at least once, in the 570s, but then things started to go wrong for him. There were two stages to Alamoundaros' demise, and they are both connected to the typical policy which the Roman state practised towards its barbarian allies. In short, such allies were only useful up to a point. When they failed, or it looked like they might threaten the state, their time was limited. Such was the case now with the Romans and Alamoundaros, and, incidentally, further to the east with the Sasanians and their Nasrid allies.

The first stage of the decline in fortune for Alamoundaros came early, when he became the target of a Roman assassination attempt. The trigger seems to have been a string of military successes, followed up by a slightly arrogant demand to Constantinople for gold so that the Jafnid leader could hire more soldiers. The Roman emperor at the time, Justin II (r. 565-578) sent a letter to a high-ranking Roman, Marcian, to have the Jafnid leader murdered. At least, he thought he did; according to John of Ephesus, a monophysite bishop who increasingly hated the Roman establishment, and who is a very partisan source for the Jafnids, the Emperor's aides bungled the letters. They sent the one ordering the assassination to Alamoundaros, and another, inviting Alamoundaros to some innocuous-sounding event where he could be easily eliminated, to Marcian. The whole thing is comically Shakespearean, and it is entirely possible that John of Ephesus made the whole thing up. But it seems that afterward, Alamoundaros quit the Roman alliance for some time, until he was encouraged to come back by a Roman agent who settled affairs at the sacred site of Resafa.

Roman intentions had been made clear, though, and not long afterwards, they had another opportunity to remove Alamoundaros – the second stage in his demise. This time, he was accused of treachery after a campaign with the senior Roman officer in the east, Maurice, turned sour. The Sasanians got wind of Roman plans, and Alamoundaros took the blame. At around the same time, he had also failed to put a smouldering dispute between rival monophysites to rest. This fatally damaged his prestige, especially since he had been specifically tasked to do so by the Emperor Tiberius II, who had succeeded Justin II in 578. Bearing in mind the premium placed on success in negotiations in tribal societies, and the standing enjoyed by the Jafnids amongst the monophysites in Jordan and Syria, this failure was a hammerblow to Alamoundaros' fortunes. The Emperor's prestige was also at stake and riding on the success of negotiations, and their failure only stoked anger amongst the highest ranks in Constantinople. As this smouldered, Maurice stormed into the imperial palace and accused Alamoundaros of betraying Roman military secrets to their sworn enemy, and from that point onwards the fate of the Jafnid leader was – sealed – especially since, by a terrible piece of bad luck, the Emperor of the moment, Tiberius II, died and Maurice become Emperor in 582. He immediately set about destroying his Jafnid rival, and in the same year, Alamoundaros was arrested, with some irony, at the consecration of a church. His son al-Numan tried to free him from house arrest and negotiate for his release, but he, too, was arrested and deposed. Alamoundaros was exiled to Sicily: there is no reason to suppose he ever returned to Syria. With him, the Jafnid lineage fell suddenly and immediately from power, and the Roman experiment with single Arab leaders, begun by Justinian, collapsed.

Alamoundaros was not the only Arab élite to suffer this fate. Since the death of al-Mundhir III in 554, the Sasanians appear to have been growing increasingly impatient with their Arab allies. The specific details are not clear, but a number of stories circulated that might explain events. Firstly, there is the possibility, even if a little unlikely, that the last Arab leader at al-Hirah, who used the common name al-Numan (the same as Alamoundaros' son, but no relation) had imprisoned the famous poet Adi ibn Zayd, a favorite of the Sasanian Emperor Khusrau II. In revenge, Khusrau had al-Numan deposed. Another story, reported by the Roman Christian writer Evagrius, held that al-Numan converted to Christianity. The Nasrids, living as they did in a Sasanian state that occasionally tolerated Christianity but did not at all support it in the way that the Romans did, had studiously avoided such open affiliation with the 'Roman' religion. They had instead steered a neutral course that allowed them to retain the loyalty and support of the Christians in al-Hirah, whom later Muslim writers asserted were present, and whose existence is confirmed by the presence of bishops from the region at ecumenical councils. Indeed, when Dhu Nuwas, the king of Himyar, asked al-Mundhir III to become involved in his persecution of Christians in the 520s, al-Mundhir III wisely refused for fear of losing an important part of his power base. So it *is* possible, that, from a Sasanian perspective, al-Numan's decision suddenly to embrace Christianity was an unwise political move, but it is not really a satisfying explanation for why Khusrau II decided to eliminate him.

The best explanation lies in a story told by Jacob of Edessa. In the political maneuverings and the rebellion that lay behind Khusrau's ascension to the Sasanian throne, the Nasrid family had backed the wrong horse. When Khusrau became Emperor, he did not forget the betrayal, and when a suitable moment arrived – triggered perhaps by the treatment of the poet Adi, or by al-Numan's unwise conversion – he decided to remove the Nasrid leaders. This is not dissimilar to the situation which occurred further west in the Roman Empire, but it is also worth mentioning James Howard-Johnston's theory that the Sasanians, who had now invaded Himyar and who were shortly to invade the Roman Empire, no longer had any need of a single client kingship based at al-Hirah. In both east and west, then, the Jafnid and Nasrid leaders faced the brutal reality of their relationship with their imperial patrons. Even if they interpreted their relationship as equal; even if they had received signals to this regard by engaging in diplomatic missions (the Nasrids also sent envoys to Abraha in 548) and in the treaty between Rome and Iran mentioned earlier; even with all of this, they were still clients of powerful empires. No matter how powerful the Jafnids and Nasrids became, the Romans and Sasanians held the final cards, and whereas in the Roman west the empire was weak and could not stand up to its German clients who, once feeble, were now militarily and politically robust, this was not the case in the east, where the armies of both states were strong and their political hierarchies firmly controlled. By 602, neither empire ran a system of Arab alliances as they had done in the previous century. Would it hurt them? Later Muslim sources describe a famous defeat of the Sasanian military by Arabs, celebrated as 'the day of Dhu Qar', sometime after 604. The great Muslim historian al-Tabari even connects this famous battle and the elimination of the Nasrids and their replacement at al-Hirah by a Sasanian agent, implying that the one led to the other, but this is debateable. Given the rapid disintegration of both the Roman and Sasanian military in the face of the Arab invasions, it is unlikely that the Jafnids or Nasrids could have made much of a difference.

5

Culture and Identity

After the emergence of Islam, the new Muslim *umma* built, over time, a sense of identity based on a range of attributes: adherence to the new religion, the dominance of Arabic as a religious and administrative language, the production of poetry, histories, and scientific knowledge, and so on. Some of these attributes have remained powerful markers of Arab identity into the modern world, particularly the use of the Arabic language to demarcate inhabitants of the Middle East from those of Europe, for example. In a similar fashion, speakers of French in Canada belong to a community with well-defined boundaries, particularly in Quebec, with political, social, and historical ramifications that often go well beyond linguistic choice. In fact, the dominance of language as a marker of 'ethnic' identity in the modern world is so powerful and familiar a phenomenon that we might wonder if the same held true in antiquity. Certainly there were linguistic choices that might define communities – the use of Greek by upper social and administrative classes in Ptolemaic

Egypt, for example, or the legal use of Greek or Latin in the Roman Empire. Without losing sight of the fundamental fact that a shared language is an important part of any group identity (if only because it allows people to communicate), we must also recognise that linguistic nationalism is a modern idea – and that there were many other factors in the ancient world that could be used to decide who was 'us' and who was 'them.'

Roman authors followed a range of ethnographic principles to demarcate barbarians. They could be non-Christians, or they might be ignorant of farming or settlement, or they might wear odd clothes (trousers gave away Germans in the capital, for example), or follow strange customs. Sometimes language *was* a part of these criteria, and we must not dismiss the comments of an earlier writer, Herodotus, in the context of resistance to the invasion of Greece by the Achaemenid king, Xerxes, of what constituted 'Greekness.' In addition to a shared religion, the great writer evoked a shared language, too. But this is very much the exception that proves the rule. Much later, in the polyglot late Roman Empire, language was just one criterion among many that could be used to define difference. We might wonder, then, where this leaves

Arabic in the pre-Islamic period. The language, after all, has gone on to assume considerable significance in the Islamic world. But what role, if any, did it play in giving Arabs 'identity' in antiquity? And what significance (if any) should we attach to the intriguing fact that it was in Roman Syria, and at the fringes of the Empire, that the form of writing we now think of as the Arabic script appears to have developed? To assess these questions, we will take a look at the evidence for the use of Arabic in the pre-Islamic Middle East, the evolution of the Arabic script, and the evidence for the production of a sort of literary tradition – the corpus of Arabic poetry which, while not written down until much later on, was originally a product of the pre-Islamic period. Taken together, could all of this have helped to constitute a type of 'pre-Islamic Arab identity?'

Old Arabic

'Old Arabic' is the name given to the oldest developmental stages of the language. Its study is confined to a small number of experts – Michael Macdonald, Laïla Nehmé, Christian Robin, and others –

and this brief overview owes a great deal to their work. (Readers who are interested in a more comprehensive and more technical overview of pic should consult the bibliography). The evidence for Old Arabic comes from a tiny group of inscriptions scattered throughout what is now Syria, Jordan, and Saudi Arabia, as well as a very small amount of literary references. This evidence suggests that Arabic remained a *spoken* language for most of the pre-Islamic period, and was not written down in the 'Arabic' script that we now associate with the language until about AD 500 – that is, very shortly before the Prophet (PBUH) received the Revelation. Before Arabic became associated with a single form of writing, it was, on the very rare occasions when it was written down, done so in scripts that were associated with other languages. The Nemara inscription, discussed above, is a famous example of this: the language is Arabic, but the script used was the form of Aramaic once employed as the 'prestige' choice for inscriptions in the Nabataean kingdom, which covered much of Jordan, northern Saudi Arabia, and southern Syria. Again, it is helpful to imagine that the letters being used to write this chapter don't exist, and all we have is Greek. The language would be English, and the grammar would be English, but it would be expressed in a totally different visual format.

The literary references to spoken Arabic come from Greco-Roman authors. St. Jerome mentions the 'Arabic sermon'; Uranius talks of the 'the language of the Arabs'; Epiphanius of Salamis (modern Famagusta, in Cyprus) mentions a goddess in the city of Petra, the old capital of the Nabataeans, who was worshipped in 'the Arabic language'; and so on. Another recent reference comes from the carbonised papyri recently uncovered at Petra, where many Arabic toponyms are sprinkled throughout the documents that the archive contains. The archive dates from the sixth century AD (i.e. 500-599).

This is, admittedly, a tiny range of material on which to base any assessment of the use and range of Arabic, and readers will immediately grasp the difficulty of understanding a problem for which a huge amount of further evidence is desirable! What about the inscriptions that also help us to understand how Arabic was used? There is a small number of examples, before 500, where Arabic is written down in other scripts. These include examples from Dedan (near al-Ula, in north-west Saudi Arabia) in the 'Dadanitic' script; from

Qaryat al-Faw in southwestern Saudi Arabia ('Sabaic' script); from the southern Nabataean city of Madain Salih, near al-Ula, in Saudi Arabia (in Nabataean script); and of course the inscription from Nemara, in Syria, also in Nabataean script. Again, these examples, all pre-dating the turn of the sixth century, show that for whatever reason, the Arabic *language* did not yet possess its own *script* and had to be written down in scripts associated with other languages.

After 500, the situation changed, and there are three inscriptions – from 512, 528/9, and 568 – that show Arabic written in the *Arabic* script, and *not* in scripts used for other languages. Studies of the new script show that it developed from the Nabataean Aramaic script, that is, the one used to write the Nemara inscription in Syria.

Arabic after 500

Recent expeditions by French and Saudi researchers, working in the northwest of Saudi Arabia, have revealed a number of Arabic inscriptions that are 'transitional' – that is, they show the different stages in the development of the Nabataean script into the Arabic one. At the same time, a couple of inscriptions that are difficult to date suggest that the Arabic script may have been used *prior* to 500. The overall picture is of a time of transition and evolution, with different forms of the script co-existing together. The cursive nature of the Arabic script means that only repeated writing on soft material (papyrus, for example) could have created the one from the other, and not, instead, chiselling letters into stone. This also therefore means that the inscriptions that have survived act only as a snapshot of what was happening, while the actual nuts and bolts of the evolution are lost to us entirely. It can easily be appreciated then that this *also* means that we can only speculate on why exactly people decided to develop a script for writing Arabic – and we shall speculate on this shortly!

What are the three sixth-century inscriptions that show a recognisably-Arabic script? The first is from Zebed in northern Syria, not far from Aleppo. It is a lintel inscription using Greek, Arabic, and Syriac, and comes from a martyrion (a shrine to a martyr) dedicated to Saint Sergius, the saint who, as noted as above, was popular with the Arabs and whose cult was patronised by the Jafnids at Resafa, east of Zebed. The Arabic does not translate the Greek and Syriac text, but is a prayer for a group of people.

The second example is the graffito discussed in Chapter Four, from Jebel Seis, also in Syria, to the southeast of Damascus. This is a remote site in the barren deserts that stretch away from the Syrian capital to the Jordanian border, and the inscription was found alongside hundreds of others at the top of an extinct volcano. The area around the volcanic crater contains a foreboding settlement and a later Islamic *qasr*, or fortified residence. It was a clearly a site of some strategic importance, with a seasonal water supply, and may have been connected by a Roman road to other settlements in the area. The graffito describes a certain Ruqaym, sent to Seis to join the garrison there by 'al-Harith the king' – that is, Arethas, the Jafnid leader. Very helpfully, Ruqaym had the presence of mind to include the date, which he scratched into the rock as the year 423 of the 'era of Bostra.' This dating mechanism, common throughout Syria and Jordan, measured time from the year when the Romans annexed the Nabataean kingdom and created the province of Arabia, whose capital was Bostra. As this had been done by the Emperor Trajan in 105/6, this provides a date of 528/9, i.e., at about the same time as Arethas was receiving his commission from Justinian. Both the language and the script are Arabic. Interestingly, the Jebel Seis example is the only secular one of these three – both Zebed, and the third, Harran, are from Christian contexts.

The Harran inscription is the third of this very small group of sixth-century Arabic inscriptions. It is dated to 463 of the era of Bostra (=568/9) and is also a martyrion, this time of St. John. The Greek and Arabic text of the inscription is rather interesting, as it provides a dedication by a certain Sharahil, son of Zalim who, in the Greek text, is described as a *phylarch*; this title was usually only given to Arab allies in the region, and while names are not always sound indicators of ethnicity, it is difficult not to notice that the name here is decidedly not Greek. Without too much fear of overstepping analytical boundaries, especially given the Arabic text, we may safely assume that Sharahil was an Arab. Studies of the text show that the Arabic part was done first, and that it differs slightly from its Greek counterpart.

Once again, we have a situation where we wish to infer a great deal from three isolated examples, and we must be careful about the conclusions that we draw.

What, then, can be said without letting our imaginations get the better of us? Firstly, it is interesting that all three of these Arabic script *and* language examples come from Roman territory, and that two of them (Zebed and Harran) are in explicitly Christian contexts. Secondly, it is also interesting that two of them (Seis and Harran) are produced by Arabs in service with, or connected to, the *phylarchate* system in the Roman Empire. Taken together, this evidence militates towards a conclusion whereby the Romans, or the relationship between the Romans and the Arabs, play or plays a role in the development of the Arabic script.

Is this plausible? It has been suggested that perhaps the bureaucratic traditions of the Roman Empire rubbed off on the Jafnids, and thus they began at their 'court' at Jabiya (presumed to be somewhere near the Golan) to write down records and so on and so forth. This writing presumably took place on the soft materials like papyrus, now lost, and thus may have been the catalyst behind the development of the script. This is an attractive proposition, but it cannot be proven either way. Similar suggestions have been made for the Nasrid court at al-Hirah in Iraq, either to do with bureaucracy or, sometimes, with the writing down of histories or of poems. Again, a nice idea, but cannot be proven.

Another interesting possibility that tallies well with the context of the Zebed and Harran inscriptions is that the Christianisation of Arab populations played a role in developing the Arabic script – that is, writing became more important due to the work of missionaries and priests who were using a text-based religion. An Arabic Bible contemporary to the pre-Islamic period would provide some support for this idea, but no such find has yet been made. There is also the counter-argument that conversion to Christianity and the practice of the religion did not require people to read or write. Indeed, one is reminded of Bede's famous story of St. Augustine, converting the Saxon kings of England and using a board with a painting of Jesus on it to do so, as they could not read! It must also be remembered that the Roman Empire had very low literacy rates, and that reading was of limited utility for the average person. So, like the bureaucratic explanation, this is also possible, but cannot be proven either way.

So where does this leave us? If we wish to avoid over-speculation, we can only conclude that we do not know precisely what caused the development of the Arabic script. This is frustrating and unsatisfying, but it is the only valid conclusion that can be drawn from the evidence. (We can only hope that more discoveries will be made in the future, although with increasing instability across the Middle East, especially in Syria, this does not seem likely.) Against this challenging analytical backdrop, however, there is some bright light. Clearly, the presence of these inscriptions and the changing nature of Arabic can be seen as a reflection of wider social and political processes – and some of these can be talked about with certainty. One such process that makes the swift transition from Roman Christian to Arab Muslim rule in the Middle East intelligible is the fact that the region was already accustomed to Arab leaders in roles of political prominence. The Romans had engaged Arabs in increasingly senior positions for some time, and now, with the Jafnids, there were clear and highly-visible models of Arab leadership in Roman Syria. The Jafnids also constituted leaders with profound religious connections, who associated themselves with the principal figures of the monophysite Christians, such as the bishop Jacob Baradaeus, and prominent cult figures, such as St.

Sergius. When Sharahil, son of Zalim, carved his name into the martyrion at Harran in 568, he did so not as a trailblazer, but as another prominent Christian Arab – a *phylarch* – in a community where this was no longer a particularly strange phenomenon. Thus, while we can only speculate if his writing in Arabic was a statement of *linguistic* identity, it seems fairly certain that we can at least read the Harran inscription, and the others, as reflections of the growing prominence of (Christian) Arabs in the polyglot, multicultural Roman world. This is especially true when it is considered that the purpose of monumental inscriptions was to set in stone for posterity (and to display to God, in the case of Christian inscriptions) the standing, status, generosity, and wealth of their dedicants. With literacy rates quite low, inscriptions were not necessarily intended to provide texts for people to read, but everyone would understand their visual language (shape, iconography, and so on), which did not require anyone to be literate.

With all of this in mind, it is noteworthy that in the mid-sixth century, an activity that had always been the preserve of the Greco-Roman urban wealthy, and that was usually done very unambiguously in the prestige language for Roman inscriptions – Latin in the west, Greek in the east – had branched out to include Arab élites, writing in Arabic. If we wish to look around for a starting point for all of this, we could cast our eyes back to the Nemara inscription in Syria, from 328, where another Arab leader, connected with both Rome and Sasanian Iran, provided an earlier snapshot of the increasing prominence of Arabs in the Roman east. In the west, Roman relations with Goths, Vandals, and Franks had empowered these 'barbarian' peoples and given them the opportunity to become political leaders of communities that also boasted deep connections to the religion of the Roman state. We can thus also see the same phenomenon playing out in the Roman east, too. It was, in the end, the Romans who helped to empower Arab political leaders through centuries of accommodation and inclusion. We will return to this point in the conclusion, below, but for now let us turn to another important cultural development taking place at the same time as the development of the Arabic script – the corpus of pre-Islamic poetry, which achieved great fame after the Muslim conquests.

Poems

One of the most useful indicators of ethnicity and ethnic or 'group' identity is the written word. Literature can be used very effectively to encode the ethos and ideology of a society, to explain its desires, its pride, its shame, what makes it different from other societies nearby, and so on. We know quite a bit, for example, about how Roman values and ideas evolved, from writers like Livy, Tacitus, and Procopius, but the Arabs did not write down any histories of themselves as a 'people' until well after the Muslim conquests. Some of the most famous of what we might now think of as 'national' histories were produced by people such as al-Tabari (whose *History of the Prophets and Kings* has now been translated into English, through a monumental effort by the State University of New York Press). These much later histories often tell us far more about the political, social, and religious concerns of the time in which they were written, than what actually may or may not have happened. This is one of the reasons, of course, why so much attention is paid to the contemporary inscriptions and sparse, externally-produced literary references to the place and role of the

Arabs in the pre-Islamic period. They constitute really the only material produced at the same time as the events that we wish to analyse.

However, while there are no contemporary written histories of the pre-Islamic Arabs, there is a substantial corpus of poetry which might, perhaps, encode some of the values of the pre-Islamic period and give us some clues as to how we might conceive Arab identity before Islam. The problem here, though, is that while experts do not question the authenticity of the product itself – in other words, they feel certain that the poems were composed during the pre-Islamic period, and are not later fabrications – the poems, and collections of poems, as we have them today were only written down a very long time after the fact. This presents a major analytical problem, because a great deal of attention was paid to this poetry by early Muslim writers, who saw in the vast array of stories a type of collective memory to be mined for their own contemporary purposes. The poems also became exemplars for Arabic grammar and composition, and achieved great fame after the seventh century, with competing collections circulating and some poems being elevated or suppressed depending on who was in power at the time. The question of transmission is also an issue, because (as the scholar Gregor Schoeler has shown) knowledge in the early Islamic period was not necessarily conveyed in either a written *or* an oral way. This means that there was no particular compelling reason to write down copies of the poems at any particular moment when they could be transmitted orally. And while there is no impediment to even extremely lengthy poems being accurately memorised and transmitted to the next generation, the later *ruwat*, or 'transmitters', of the pre-Islamic poems often fixed broken or 'crooked' elements of grammar and rhyme as poems were memorised and 'bettered' for future dissemination.

A healthy scepticism is in order, then, but at the same time, it should not take away the fact that these poems surely played a part in creating ideas about the identity of different tribal groupings and perhaps, overall, an idea of 'Arabness' based on a set of shared attributes or characteristics. The problem lies in knowing what to safely accept or reject – a monumental task! This job is made more difficult by the fact that both the Jafnid and Nasrid dynasties were said by Muslim writers to have patronised poetry at Jabiya and al-Hirah, and if poems were written down under the auspices of these leaders as some have claimed (but without adducing any evidence) then this also becomes another possible catalyst for the development of the Arabic script. If we look carefully at the poems, some feature historically-verifiable figures and places, and individual poems have been used effectively by scholars to illuminate contemporary events, like the famous plague which occurred during the time of Justinian. Many poems include catalogues of tribes and political groupings known to have existed in the pre-Islamic period, and talk of places and other events which can be verified. But sometimes there are hopelessly tangled problems; a brief example will suffice to show the difficulties we face in using these poems as historical artefacts.

Perhaps the most famous author to appear in one of the well-known poetry collections, the *Mu'allaqat*, is Imru al-Qays from the tribe of Kinda (no relation to the Imru al-Qays of Nemara). Imru al-Qays is connected with poems that address the death of his father, and his subsequent quest for vengeance. In one poem, he travels to Constantinople to try and obtain the support of Justinian. For the Roman historian, elements of the story bear a striking resemblance to the annals of Roman diplomatic forays into Arabia, as they are covered by Procopius and Nonnosus (see ch. 3, above). Procopius describes a certain Qays/Kaisos (Imru al-Qays?) as the Roman choice for leadership over the 'Maddene Saracens' – that is, Ma'add, the arena of Roman/Sasanian proxy competition in central-northern Arabia. In the version given by Nonnosus, Kays also travels to the Roman capital to visit Justinian! But none of this means that the poem and the autobiography of Nonnosus are describing the same events. The name Imru al-Qays is common, and belongs to not just one, but a range of different ancient poets. More problematically, a proliferation of later legends about Imru al-Qays casts further uncertainty over the association between the stories in the poems and those told by Procopius and Nonnosus. (One might think here about the problems involved in separating the 'historical' King Arthur from the mythical one – a difficult, if not totally impossible, task). In short, even where things appear to line up, it is important not to jump to conclusions and treat the poems as accurate sources for the history of the pre-Islamic period.

Does this mean that the poems are useless for the historian? No; we should pay attention to the form, not the content. Like the Homeric epics and other famous oral poems in history, the production of the material represents a form of culture-creation, even if the 'final product' is far-removed from the original composition. Thus the authenticity of the *form* is not in question. For the pre-Islamic poems, there is a consensus among scholars that the poems were produced in a geographically-defined area in the pre-Islamic period. In common with the inscriptions discussed above, then, perhaps the best question we can ask of this literary product is what other social or political processes it might be reflecting. If the inscriptions reflect the growing prominence of Arab élites vis-à-vis the Roman Empire and the emergence of a powerful 'Arab' political and religious stratum in Roman society, what does the poetry represent? Asking this question allows us to bypass some of the unanswerable questions which litter the analytical landscape. We followed the same procedure with the inscriptions – we don't know if the Nemara inscription really says 'king of all the Arabs', and even if it does, what that means. But it *does* show political power and position, and represents an important snapshot in the growth of Arab élites before the Muslim conquests.

Similarly, with the poems, we need not concern ourselves with the differences between the sixth- and eighth-century versions, or with the question of whether a certain figure may or may not have existed. Let us instead return to the problem with which this chapter began – the link between language, culture, and identity. We cannot say with any confidence what sort of identities the poems helped to create – so we do not know if they created feelings of pan-Arabness or unity between different tribes. But what is very interesting and noteworthy is that the production of the poetry did not happen in a vacuum. In fact, throughout the sixth century, three important things were happening simultaneously. A corpus of Arabic poetry was being created. The Arabic script was developing. And the world controlled by the empires of Rome and Sasanian Iran witnessed the emergence of powerful Arab élites, who played, at least in the case of the Jafnids (the sources for the Nasrids are very poor) significant roles in the community life of the regions where they lived. There were surely other Arab élites involved in this process as well, but our sources do not talk about them.

The conclusion we might draw, then, is of great significance: that it was in the multicultural and vibrant late antique world, dominated by the last two superpowers of antiquity, that a greater Arab political, cultural, and religious consciousness emerged, and was expressed for some of the time in Arabic, and not Greek. Even if the specifics of how all of this happened, and what the catalysts were for script development (for example) are hidden from us, we should not ignore an important fact: many of the attributes or markers crucial for later ideas about Arab identity – literature, language, political and religious prominence – were alive and well before the seventh century. Most, if not all, held some kind of link to the wider relationship between Romans, Iranians, and Arabs, and this is why the history of the Arabs before Islam is also part of the history of Rome and Iran, and a vitally important part, too, of world history.

6

Continuity and change

In the first part of the seventh century, the Sasanian Emperor Khusrau II launched a massive invasion of the Roman Empire. The trigger was the assassination of the Roman Emperor Maurice, who had helped Khusrau II to the Sasanian throne, and his replacement in Constantinople by a new Emperor, Phocas, whom Khusrau seems to have viewed as a choice target. Because treaties and agreements in the ancient world were interpersonal, with the death of his former ally Maurice, Khusrau felt no obligation to stick to peace with the Romans. On the contrary, it seemed like an opportune moment to invade the Roman Empire, and perhaps to execute whatever long-held ambition the Sasanians may have nurtured to win back all that their Achaemenid predecessors had lost to Alexander the Great.

The 'world-crisis' that followed has been recently examined in marvellous detail by James Howard-Johnston. In short, the Sasanians succeeded in occupying large parts of Roman territory for nearly a generation, before a resurgence began under a man named Heraclius, who deposed the feeble Phocas in 610. Heraclius is better known to history, though, as the Roman Emperor who ceded Syria to the Muslim armies. What is usually forgotten is his masterful and incredible victory over Khusrau, falling on the Sasanian reserves at Nineveh in Iraq while Khusrau and his Balkan Avar allies were tied up near Constantinople, imagining that they were themselves close to a final and stunning triumph. By the time that Khusrau realised that his supply lines had been cut, and that his adversary was running rampant in the heart of the Sasanian Empire, he could no longer sustain his position and was soon eliminated by a cabal of his own nobles. Heraclius basked in Roman glory; he had even regained the True Cross, snatched from Jerusalem by the victorious Sasanians, and all seemed well for the Empire. But by 636, after the stunning Muslim victory over the Roman army by the Yarmuk River in Jordan, the Roman Empire was truncated to Constantinople and the Balkans, the Near East entered a new phase of its history, and the Sasanian Empire, almost in its entirety, was lost to the invaders from Arabia. It is said that Heraclius bid a tearful farewell to Syria, saying that no

Byzantine man would ever see it again until the coming of the anti-Christ.

This is not the place to examine the Muslim conquests in detail: interested readers should consult the excellent works covering this topic by scholars such as Hugh Kennedy and Fred Donner. But one of the goals of this short work is to emphasise the history of the Arabs in the pre-Islamic period within the wider schemes of world history: the history of the Roman and Sasanian Empires, and a broad geographical canvas that stretched from the Yemeni coast all the way to northern Mesopotamia and Turkey. Thus, what we should do, in closing, is to connect the history of the Arabs discussed in this short volume to what came afterwards. The period we now know as the 'Muslim Conquests' effected many significant changes, but also picked up on and sometimes accelerated existing political, social, and religious phenomena. One very important aspect of the Roman Empire in the sixth century, from the perspective of the historical problem of 'continuity and change', was the presence of Arab political leaders in positions of considerable political and social authority – individuals such as the Jafnids Arethas and Alamoundaros, the leaders of the Hujrid family, and al-

Mundhir III of the Nasrids. Figures such as these would be the norm later as Muslim Arabs became the political masters of the Near East, rather than Christian or pagan Arabs. It is thus something of a myth that the conquests 'Arabised' the Middle East, because Arab populations and élites were clearly being empowered well beforehand within the framework of the opportunities provided by Rome, Himyar, and Iran. The rise of people like Arethas was partly dependent on Roman support, just as, in the west, Germanic barbarian leaders had catapulted themselves into positions of significant power by tapping into the bureaucratic, military, and social ladders of the Empire's structure. While we know far less about the relationship between the Nasrids and the Sasanians – this short book necessarily focuses on the Roman side of things – it is reasonable to imagine that similar processes were underway at al-Hirah in Iraq.

Through all of this, therefore, the two empires had thus helped to create a sense of what was possible, and, in turn, laid the groundwork in places like Syria and Iraq for Arab leadership to become a normal part of community and political life. It must be remembered that people like Arethas were not simply political agents affiliated with imperial patrons, but also fulfilled vital community roles through their association with holy men such as Jacob Baradeus, and through their support of religious centres such as monasteries and the churches of St. Sergius. They were community leaders. The Jafnids were also linked to secular activities such as the construction of non-religious buildings in Syria and Jordan, and so spanned the range of political, military, religious, and secular functions. Years ago, the Byzantinist Mark Whittow evoked the possibility that the Jafnids had foreshadowed one of the great achievements of the Muslim invasions by uniting the manpower of the tribe with the wealth of the settled lands of the Fertile Crescent. In creating the Muslim *umma*, the Umayyad, and then the Abbasid caliphates, provided a unity to the Middle East that had never quite existed before. But what if a prototype of the most important part of this, the union of the tribes and the Fertile Crescent, had already been underway in the sixth century? Taken from this perspective, then, it can be seen that the arrival of a *new kind* of Arab political and religious leadership was not so much of a drastic change as it might seem, because the communities of the Near East were already well-accustomed to Arab leaders who played both political and religious roles, and who bridged the divide between desert and settled lands, and between tribe and state. The unity between these different aspects of late antique culture was eased by religion – Islam later, but Christianity beforehand, especially as the Jafnids seem to have rather effectively translated their traditional function as tribal mediators into the realm of ecclesiastical politics. For their part, the Nasrids at al-Hirah stayed decidedly aloof from religious problems, acting as a sort of inclusive umbrella leadership to the multifaith components of Hiran society. Arab leaders were then, in one way, a normal part of the multicultural, pre-Islamic Middle East, as they would be later, in higher profile, a part of the multicultural, post-Islamic world. It is instructive that stories of the capture of Damascus during the Muslim invasions featured fifth-columnists, who saw the recently-returned Romans as more of a threat than the Arab invaders, with whom they had some form of (political? social? religious?) affinity.

Finally, from a religious perspective, while the new Islamic religion was a powerful and highly successful universalising force, the religious landscape of the sixth and seventh centuries in the Roman *and*

Sasanian empires was of considerable diversity. The dominance of Islam in the modern Middle East was a position achieved over time, and the introduction of a new form of a religion of the Book – an Abrahamic religion – into an area where other forms of the religion of the Book already existed, thus formed another natural layer of continuity at the very beginning. Thus while the Muslim Conquests as historical phenomenon were no doubt drastic and quick if one was caught up in a particular battle or other violent event, from the macrohistorical view, we have a very different picture indeed, and one in which the characters and processes examined here played a small, but important, role.

References and Further Reading

The subject covered here touches on a wide and intersecting range of disciplines. For those readers interested in delving deeper, a list of suggested reading is included here.

N. Abbott, *The Rise of the North Arabian Script and its Kura'nic Development, With a Full Description of the Kura'nic Manuscripts in the Oriental Institute* (Chicago, 1939).

A.R. al-Ansary, *Qaryat al-Faw: A Portrait of Pre-Islamic Civilisation in Sa'udi Arabia* (Riyadh, 1982).

A.J. Arberry, *The Seven Odes. The First Chapter in Arabic Literature* (London, 1957).

P. Athanassiadi and M. Frede (eds.), *Pagan Monotheism in Late Antiquity* (Oxford, 1999)

A. al-Azmeh, *Muslim Kingship. Power and the Sacred in Muslim, Christian and Pagan Polities* (London, 1997).

E.B. Banning, 'Peasants, pastoralists, and the *pax romana*', *Bulletin of the American Schools of Oriental Research*, 261 (1986), 25-50.

F. Barth, *Nomads of South Persia. The Basseri Tribe of the Khamseh Confederacy* (Oslo, 1961).

A.F.L. Beeston, 'Nemāra and Faw', *Bulletin of the School of Oriental and African Studies*, 42/1 (1979), 1-6.

A.F.L. Beeston, T.M. Johnstone, R.B. Serjeant, and G.R. Smith, (eds.) *Arabic Literature to the End of the Umayyad Period* (Cambridge, 1983).

R. Blachère, *Histoire de la littérature arabe des origines à la fin du XVe siècle ap. J.-C.*, 3 vols (Paris, 1952-1964).

R. Blockley, *East Roman Foreign Policy. Formation and Conduct from Diocletian to Anastasius* (Leeds, 1992).

C. Bosworth, 'Iran and the Arabs Before Islam', in E. Yarshater, (ed.), *The Cambridge History of Iran,* iii/i: *The Seleucid, Parthian and Sasanian Periods* (Cambridge, 1983), 593-612.

G. Bowersock, P. Brown and O. Grabar (eds.), *Interpreting Late Antiquity. Essays on the Postclassical World* (Cambridge, Mass., 2001).

Averil Cameron, B. Ward-Perkins, and M. Whitby (eds.), *The Cambridge Ancient History*, xiv: *Late Antiquity: Empire and Successors, AD 425-600* (Cambridge, 2000).

Averil Cameron, *The Mediterranean World in Late Antiquity*, 2nd edn. (London, 2011).

M. Canepa, *The Two Eyes of the Earth. Art and Ritual of Kingship Between Rome and Sasanian Iran* (Berkeley, 2009).

D.F. Caner, *History and Hagiography from the Late Antique Sinai* (Liverpool, 2010).

H. Cotton, R. Hoyland, J. Price, and D. Wasserstein (eds.), *From Hellenism to Islam: Cultural and Linguistic Change in the Roman Near East* (Cambridge, 2009).

P. Crone, *Meccan Trade and the Rise of Islam* (Princeton, 1987).

———, *Slaves on Horses. The Evolution of the Islamic Polity* (Cambridge, 1980).

P. Crone and Cook, M., *Hagarism. The Making of the Islamic World* (Cambridge, 1977).

V.S. Curtis and S. Stewart (eds.), *The Idea of Iran*, iii: *The Sasanian Era* (London, 2008).

T. Daryaee, *Sasanian Persia. The Rise and Fall of an Empire* (London, 2009).

B. Dignas, and E. Winter, *Rome and Persia in Late Antiquity. Neighbours and Rivals* (Cambridge, 2007).

F.M. Donner, *The Early Islamic Conquests* (Princeton, 1981).

———, *Narratives of Islamic Origins. The Beginnings of Islamic Historical Writing* (Princeton, 1998).

A.A. Duri, *The Rise of Historical Writing Among the Arabs*, trans. L. Conrad (Princeton, 1983).

G. Fisher, 'A new perspective on Rome's desert frontier', *Bulletin of the American Schools of Oriental Research*, 336 (2004), 49-60.

———, *Between Empires. Arabs, Romans, and Sasanians in Late Antiquity* (Oxford, 2011).

———, 'From Mavia to al-Mundhir: Arab Christians and Arab tribes in the late Roman east', in I. Toral Niehoff and K. Dimitriev (eds.), *Religious Culture in Late Antique Arabia* (Brill, forthcoming).

———, 'Kingdoms or dynasties? Arabs, history, and identity in the last century before Islam', *Journal of Late Antiquity* 4/2 (2011), 245-267.

———, 'The political development of the Ghassān between Rome and Iran', *Journal of Late Antiquity*, 1/2 (2008), 313-36.

———, 'The politics of religion. Arabs, Christians, and Romans in the last century before Islam', in R. Acar, B. Bas, and T. Kirby (eds.), *Philosophy and the Abrahamic Religions: Scriptural Hermeneutics and Epistemology* (Cambridge, 2012), 81-94.

C. Foss, 'Syria in transition, A.D. 550-750: an archaeological approach', *Dumbarton Oaks Papers,* 51 (1997).

E.K. Fowden, *The Barbarian Plain: Saint Sergius between Rome and Iran* (Berkeley, 1999)

G. Fowden, *Empire to Commonwealth: Consequences of Monotheism in Late Antiquity* (Princeton, 1993).

G. Fowden and E.K. Fowden, *Studies on Hellenism, Christianity and the Umayyads* (Paris, 2004).

P. Freeman and D. Kennedy (eds.), *The Defence of the Roman and Byzantine East: Proceedings of a Colloquium held at the University of Sheffield in April 1986*, 2 vols, (Oxford, 1986).

W.H.C. Frend, *The Rise of the Monophysite Movement. Chapters in the History of the Church in the Fifth and Sixth Centuries* (Cambridge, 1972).

I. Gajda, *Le royaume de Ḥimyar à l'époque monothéiste* (Paris, 2009).

D. Genequand, 'Some thoughts on Qasr al-Hayr al Gharbi, its dam, its monastery and the Ghassanids', *Levant*, 38 (2006), 63-84.

J. van Ginkel, 'John of Ephesus. A Monophysite Historian in Sixth Century Byzantium', D. Litt. Thesis, Rijksuniversiteit Groningen, 1995.

D. Graf, 'The Saracens and the defense of the Arabian frontier', *Bulletin of the American Schools of Oriental Research*, 229 (1978), 1-26.

G. Greatrex, *Rome and Persia at War, 502-532* (Leeds, 1998).

G. Greatrex and S. Lieu (eds.), *The Roman Eastern Frontier and the Persian Wars, AD 363-628* (London, 2007).

G. Greatrex and S. Mitchell (eds.), *Ethnicity and Culture in Late Antiquity* (London, 2000).

B. Gruendler, *The Development of the Arabic Scripts. From the Nabataean Era to the First Islamic Century According to Dated Texts* (Atlanta, 1993).

F. K. Haarer, *Anastasius I. Politics and Empire in the Late Roman World* (Cambridge, 2006).

T. Hainthaler, *Christliche Araber vor dem Islam* (Leuven, 2007).

T. Holland, *In the Shadow of the Sword. Global Empire and the Rise of a New Religion* (London, 2012).

K.G. Holum and H. Lapin (eds.), *Shaping the Middle East. Jews, Christians, and Muslims in an Age of Transition, 400-800 C.E.* (Bethesda, 2011).

J. Howard-Johnston, *East Rome, Sasanian Persia, and the End of Antiquity* (Aldershot, 2006).

_____, *Witnesses to a World Crisis. Historians and Histories of the Middle East in the Seventh Century* (Oxford, 2011).

R. Hoyland, *Arabia and the Arabs. From the Bronze Age to the Coming of Islam* (London, 2001).

———, 'Late Roman Provincia Arabia, Monophysite Monks and Arab tribes: a problem of centre and periphery', *Semitica et Classica*, 2, 117-39.

———, *Seeing Islam as Others Saw It. A Survey and Evaluation of Christian, Jewish and Zoroastrian Writings on Early Islam* (Princeton, 1997).

R.S. Humphreys, *Islamic History. A Framework for Inquiry* (Rev edn, London, 1991).

B. Isaac, *The Limits of Empire: The Roman Army in the East* (2nd edn, Oxford, 1990).

A. Jones, *Early Arabic Poetry*, 2 vols (Reading, 1992-1996).

D. Kennedy, *The Roman Army in Jordan* (London, 2004).

H. Kennedy, *The Prophet and the Age of the Caliphates. The Islamic Near East from the Sixth to the Eleventh Century* (2nd edn, London, 2004).

A. Khazanov, *Nomads and the Outside World* (2nd edn, Madison, 1994).

P.S. Khoury and J. Kostiner (eds.), *Tribes and State Formation in the Middle East* (Berkeley, 1990).

W. Lancaster and F. Lancaster, 'Concepts of leadership in bedouin society', in J. Haldon and L.

Conrad (eds.), *The Byzantine and Early Islamic Near East*, vi: *Élites Old and New in the Byzantine and Early Islamic Near East* (Princeton, 2004), 29-61.

A. D. Lee, *Information and Frontiers. Roman Foreign Relations in Late Antiquity* (Cambridge, 1993).

N. Lenski, (ed.), *The Cambridge Companion to the Age of Constantine* (Cambridge, 2006).

———, 'Captivity and slavery among the Saracens in late antiquity (CA. 250-630 CE)', *Antiquité Tardive* 19 (2011), 237-266.

A. Lewin, 'Amr ibn Adi, Mavia, the phylarchs and the late Roman army: peace and war in the Near East', in A. Lewin and P. Pellegrini (eds.), *The Late Roman Army in the Near East from Diocletian to the Arab Conquest. Proceedings of a Colloquium held at Potenza, Acerenza, and Matera, Italy (May 2005)* (Oxford, 2007), 243-262.

E. Luttwak, *The Grand Strategy of the Roman Empire* (Baltimore, 1976).

———, *The Grand Strategy of the Byzantine Empire* (Cambridge, Mass., 2009).

C.J. Lyall (ed.), *The Mufaddaliyat. An Anthology of Ancient Arabian Odes Complied by Al Mufaddal son of Muḥammad, according to the recension and with the commentary of Abu Muhammad Al-Qasim ibn Muhammad al-Anbari*,3 vols (Oxford, 1918).

M. Maas (ed.), *The Cambridge Companion to the Age of Justinian* (Cambridge, 2005).

M.C.A. Macdonald, 'Arabs, Arabias, and Arabic before Late Antiquity', *Topoi*, 16/1 (2009), 277-332.

———, *The Development of Arabic as a Written Language* (Oxford, 2010).

———, *Literacy and Identity in Pre-Islamic Arabia* (Farnham, 2009).

———, 'Reflections on the linguistic map of Pre-Islamic Arabia', *Arabian Archaeology and Epigraphy*, 11/1 (2000), 28-79.

M.V. McDonald, 'Orally transmitted poetry in pre Islamic Arabia and other pre-literate societies', *Journal of Arabic Literature*, 9 (1978), 14-31.

V. Menze, *Justinian and the Making of the Syrian Orthodox Church* (Oxford, 2008).

P. Mayerson, 'Saracens and Romans: Micro-macro relationships', *Bulletin of the American Schools of Oriental Research*, 274 (1989), 71-79.

F. Millar, 'Christian monasticism in Roman Arabia at the birth of Mahomet', *Semitica et Classica* 2 (2009), 97-115.

———, 'The evolution of the Syrian Orthodox Church in the pre-Islamic period: from Greek to Syriac', *Journal of Early Christian Studies*, forthcoming.

———, 'Hagar, Ishmael, Josephus and the origins of Islam', *Journal of Jewish Studies*, 44/1 (1993), 23-45.

———, 'Rome's Arab allies in late antiquity. Conceptions and representations from within the frontiers of the empire', in H. Börm and J. Wiesehöfer (eds.), *Commutatio et Contentio. Studies in the Late Roman, Sasanian, and Early Islamic Near East in Memory of Zeev Rubin* (Düsseldorf, 2010), 199-226

———, *The Roman Near East. 31 BC – AD 337* (Cambridge, Mass., 2001).

———, 'A Syriac Codex from near Palmyra and the 'Ghassanid' Abokarib', *Hugoye*, forthcoming.

M. Mir (ed.), *Literary Heritage of Classical Islam* (Princeton, 1993).

M. Mundy and B. Musallam (eds.), *The Transformation of Nomadic Society in the Arab East* (Cambridge, 2000).

L. Nehmé, 'A glimpse of the development of the Nabataean script into Arabic based on new and old material' in M.C.A. Macdonald (ed.), *The Development of Arabic as a Written Language* (Oxford, 2010).

G. Olinder, *The Kings of Kinda of the Family of Akil al Murār* (Leipzig, 1927).

S.T. Parker, *Romans and Saracens. A History of the Arabian Frontier* (Winona Lake, 1986).

M. Piccirillo, 'The church of Saint Sergius at Nitl. A centre of the Christian Arabs in the steppe at the gates of Madaba', *Liber Annuus*, 51 (2001), 267-284.

W. Pohl (ed.), *Kingdoms of the Empire. The Integration of Barbarians in Late Antiquity* (Leiden, 1997).

W. Pohl, I. Wood, and H. Reimitz, (eds.), *The Transformation of Frontiers: from Late Antiquity to the Carolingians* (Leiden, 2001).

A. Poidebard, *La Trace de Rome dans le désert de Syrie: Le Limes de Trajan à la conquête arabe. Recherches aériennes (1925-1932)* (Paris, 1934).

P. Pourshariati, *Decline and Fall of the Sasanian Empire. The Sasanian-Parthian Confederacy and the Arab Conquest of Iran* (London, 2008).

Reynolds, G. S. (ed.), *The Qur'ān in its Historical Context* (London, 2008).

J. Retsö, *The Arabs in Antiquity: Their History from the Assyrians to the Umayyads* (New York, 2003).

C. Robin (ed.), *L'Arabie antique de Karab'il à Mahomet: nouvelles données sur l'histoire des Arabes grâce aux inscriptions* (Aix-en Provence, 1991).

———, 'Les Arabes de Himyar, des <<Romains>> et des Perses (IIIe-VIe siècles de l'ère chrétienne)', *Semitica et Classica*,1 (2008), 167-208.

———, 'Les inscriptions de l'Arabie antique et les études arabes', *Arabica*, 48 (2001), 509-577.

———, 'La réforme de l'écriture arabe à l'époque du califat médinois', *Mélanges de l'Université Saint Joseph*, 56 (2006), 319-364.

———, 'Le royaume Hujride, dit <<royaume de Kinda>>, entre Himyar et Byzance', *Comptes Rendue de l'Academie des Inscriptions et Belles Lettres*(1996), 665-714.

C. Robin and Y. Calvet, *Arabie heureuse, Arabie déserte. Les antiquités arabiques du Musée du Louvre* (Paris, 1997).

C. Robin and D. Genequand (eds.), *Regards croisés de l'histoire et de l'archéologie sur la dynastie Jafnide*, forthcoming.

C. Robin and M. Gorea, 'Un réexamen de l'inscription arabe préislamique du Gabal Usays (528-529 É. Chr.)', *Arabica*, 49 (2002), 503-510.

C. Robin and J. Schiettecatte, J. (eds.), *L'Arabie à la veille de l'Islam. Bilan Clinique* (Paris, 2009).

C. Robinson, *Empire and Élites after the Muslim Conquest. The Transformation of Northern Mesopotamia* (Cambridge, 2000).

A. van Roey and P. Allen (eds.), *Monophysite Texts of the Sixth Century* (Leuven, 1994).

G. Rothstein, *Die Dynastie der Laḥmiden in al-Ḥira. Ein Versuch zur arabisch-persischen Geschichte zur Zeit der Sasaniden* (Berlin, 1899).

Z. Rubin, 'Byzantium and Southern Arabia – the policy of Anastasius', in D.H. French and C.S. Lightfoot (eds.), *The Eastern Frontier of the Roman Empire. Proceedings of a Colloquium Held at Ankara in September 1988,* 2 vols (Oxford, 1989), ii, 383-420.

———, 'Diplomacy and war in the relations between Byzantium and the Sassanids in the fifth century AD', in P. Freeman and D. Kennedy (eds.), *The Defence of the Roman and Byzantine East: Proceedings of a Colloquium held at the University of Sheffield in April 1986,* 2 vols (Oxford, 1986), ii, 677-695.

P.C. Salzman, *Pastoralists. Equality, Hierarchy, and the State* (Boulder, 2004).

P. Sarris, *Empires of Faith. The Fall of Rome and the Rise of Islam, 500-700.*

M. Sartre, *Bostra. Des origins à l'Islam* (Paris, 1985).

———, *Trois études sur l'Arabie romaine et byzantine* (Brussels, 1982)

R. Schick, *The Christian Communities of Palestine from Byzantine to Islamic Rule* (Princeton, 1995).

G. Schoeler, *The Genesis of Literature in Islam. From the Aural to the Read*, trans. S.M. Toorawa (Edinburgh, 2002).

———, *The Oral and the Written in Early Islam*, trans. U. Vagelpohl, ed. J.E. Montgomery (London, 2006).

J.B. Segal, 'Arabs in Syriac literature before the rise of Islam', *Jerusalem Studies in Arabic and Islam*, 4 (1984), 89-124.

M.A. Sells, *Desert Tracings. Six Classic Arabian Odes by 'Alqama, Shanfara, Labid, 'Antara, Al-A'sha and Dhu al-Rumma* (Middletown, CT., 1989).

I. Shahid, 'Byzantium and the Arabs during the reign of Constantine: the Namāra inscription', B*yzantinische Forschungen*, 26 (2000), 81-86.

———, *Byzantium and the Arabs in the Fifth Century* (Washington, 1989).

———, *Byzantium and the Arabs in the Sixth Century*, 2 vols (Washington, 1995, 2002, 2010).

———, *Rome and the Arabs. A Prolegomenon to the Study of Byzantium and the Arabs* (Washington, 1984).

B.D. Shaw, ' 'Eaters of Flesh, Drinkers of Milk': The Ancient Mediterranean ideology of the pastoral nomad', *Ancient Society*, 13-14 (1982), 5-31.

S. Smith 'Events in Arabia in the 6th century A.D.', *Bulletin of the School of Oriental and African Studies*, 16/3 (1954), 425-468.

J. Szuchman, *Nomads, Tribes, and the State in the Ancient Near East. Cross Disciplinary Perspectives* (Chicago, 2008).

Al-Tabari. *The History of al-Tabari, v. The Sāsānids, the Byzantines, the Lakhmids, and Yemen*, trans. And comm. C. E. Bosworth (Albany, 1999).

R. Tapper (ed.), *The Conflict of Tribe and State in Iran and Afghanistan* (London, 1983).

I. Toral-Niehoff, 'The ʿIbād of al-Ḥīra: an Arab Christian community in late antique Iraq', in A. Neuwirth, M. Marx, and N. Sinai (eds.), *The Qur'an in Context – Entangled Histories and Textual Palimpsests* (Leiden, 2010), 323-347.

J.S. Trimingham, *Christianity Among the Arabs in Pre Islamic Times* (New York, 1979).

C.G. Tuetey, *Imrualkais of Kinda, Poet. Circa A. D. 500-535. The Poems– The Life – the Background* (London, 1977).

K. Versteegh and M. Eid (eds.), *Encyclopedia of Arabic Language and Linguistics*, 4 vols, (Leiden, 2006-2008).

J. Walker, *The Legend of Mar Qardagh. Narrative and Christian Heroism in Late Antique Iraq* (Berkeley, 2006).

A. Walmsley, *Early Islamic Syria. An Archaeological Assessment* (London, 2007).

C.R. Whittaker, *Frontiers of the Roman Empire. A Social and Economic Study* (Baltimore, 1994).

M. Whittow, *The Making of Byzantium, 600-1025* (Berkeley, 1996).

———, 'Rome and the Jafnids: writing the history of a 6th-c. tribal dynasty', in J.   Humphrey (ed.), *The Roman and Byzantine Near East: Some Recent Archaeological* Research, 3 vols, Portsmouth, R.I., 1995-2002), ii, 207-224.

C. Wickham, *Framing the Early Middle Ages: Europe and the Mediterranean 400-800* (Oxford, 2005).

J. Wiesehöfer, *Ancient Persia. From 550 BC to 650 AD*, trans. A. Azodi (London, 1996).

P. Wood, *We Have No King But Christ. Christian Political Thought in Greater Syria on the Eve of the Arab Conquest (c.400-585)* (Oxford, 2010).

P. Yule, *Himyar. Spätantike im Jemen. Late Antique Yemen* (Aichwald, 2007).

M.J. Zwettler, 'Maʿadd in Late-ancient Arabian epigraphy and other pre-Islamic sources', *Wiener Zeitschrift für die Kunde des Morgenlandes*, 90 (2000), 223-309.

Printed in Great Britain
by Amazon.co.uk, Ltd.,
Marston Gate.